Food Stories
from
The Bible

J.O. Terry

Revised Edition

*Stories of God's Providence to
Feed the Physical and Spiritual
Hunger of Humankind*

Food Stories from the Bible
Revised Edition
© J.O.Terry
Fort Worth
2009

Stories are verbatim or adapted from the New International Version of the Bible. The stories are worded as suggested presentations for telling. Storyers are encouraged to use Bible versions and translations common to their listeners and not translations of these model stories.

ISBN 978-0-9825079-0-2

Resources: Church Starting Network
Church Starting and Growth
English

Daniel R. Sánchez, Ebbie C. Smith, and Curtis Watke, *Starting Reproducing Congregations: A Guidebook for Contextual New Church Development.* Ft. Worth, Texas: Church Starting Network, 2001. (www.churchstarting.net)

Daniel R. Sánchez, Ebbie C. Smith, and Curtis Watke. *Starting Reproducing Congregations Strategy Planner: A Workbook for Contextual New Church Development.* Ft. Worth, Texas: Church Starting Network, 2001. (www.churchstarting.net)

Ebbie C. Smith, *Growing Healthy Churches: New Directions for Church Growth in the 21st Century.* Ft. Worth, Texas: Church Starting Network, 2003. (www.churchstarting.net)

Daniel R. Sánchez & Rudolph González. *Sharing the Good News with Our Roman Catholic Friends.* Ft. Worth, Texas: Church Starting Network, 2004. (www.churchstarting.net)

Daniel R. Sánchez, *Gospel in the Rosary.* Ft. Worth, Texas: Church Starting Network, 2004. (www.churchstarting.net)

Ebbie C. Smith. *Spiritual Warfare for 21st Century Christians.* Ft. Worth, Texas: Church Starting Network, 2005. (www.churchstarting.net)

Daniel R. Sánchez, ed., *Church Planting Movements in North America.* Ft. Worth, Texas: Church Starting Network, 2007. (www.churchstarting.net)

Daniel R. Sánchez, *Hispanic Realities Impacting America: Implications for Evangelism and Missions*. Ft. Worth, Texas: Church Starting Network, 2006. (www.churchstarting.net)

Ebbie C. Smith, *Basic Churches are Real Churches*. Ft. Worth, Texas: Church Starting Network, 2009. (www.churchstarting.net)

Spanish

Daniel R. Sánchez, Ebbie C. Smith, and Curtis Watke, *Como Sembrar Iglesias en el Siglo XXI*. El Paso, Texas: Casa Bautista de Publicaciones, 2001. www.sembrariglesias.net (www.churchstarting.net)

Daniel R. Sánchez, Ebbie C. Smith, and Curtis Watke, *Mis Planes Estratégicos Para Sembrar Iglesias en El Siglo XXI: Libro de trabajo para el desarrollo contextual de una iglesia nueva*. Ft. Worth, Texas: Church Starting Network, 2002. www.sembrariglesias.net (www.churchstarting.net)

Daniel R. Sánchez, Ebbie C. Smith, *Cultivando Iglesias Saludables*. Ft. Worth, Texas: Church Starting Network, 2008. www.sembrariglesias.net (www.churchstarting.net)

Daniel R. Sánchez, Rodolfo González. *Comparta Las Buenas Nuevas Con Sus Amigos Católicos*. Ft. Worth, Texas: Church Starting Network, 2004. www.sembrariglesias.net (www.churchstarting.net)

Daniel R. Sánchez. *Evangelio En El Rosario*. Ft. Worth, Texas: Church Starting Network, 2004. www.sembrariglesias.net (www.churchstarting.net)

Daniel R. Sánchez. *Iglesia: Crecimiento y Cultura*. Ft. Worth, Texas: Church Starting Network, 2004. www.sembrariglesias.net (www.churchstarting.net)

Daniel R. Sánchez. *Manual para Implementar Crecimiento y Cultura*. Ft. Worth, Texas: Church Starting Network, 2004. www.sembrariglesias.net (www.churchstarting.net)

Daniel R. Sánchez. *Realidades Hispanas Que Impactan A América: Implicaciones para Evangelización y Misiones.* Ft. Worth, Texas: Church Starting Network, 2006. www.sembrariglesias.net (www.churchstarting.net)

J.O. Terry, *Guía Para La Narrativa Bíblica* (Synopsis of the Bible Storying Handbook, translated into Spanish by Keith Stamps). Ft. Worth, Texas: Church Starting Network, 2008. www.sembrariglesias.net (www.churchstarting.net)

Bible Storying Resources

J.O Terry, *Basic Bible Storying*. Ft. Worth, Texas: Church Starting Network, 2006. (www.churchstarting.net)

Daniel R. Sánchez, J.O. Terry, LaNette Thompson. *Bible Storying for Church Planting*. Ft. Worth, Texas: Church Starting Network, 2008. (www.churchstarting.net)

J.O. Terry, *Bible Storying Handbook: For Short-Term Church Mission Teams and Mission Volunteers.* Ft. Worth, Texas: Church Starting Network, 2008. (www.churchstarting.net)

J.O. Terry, *Guía Para La Narrativa Bíblica* (Synopsis of the Bible Storying Handbook, translated into Spanish by Keith Stamps). Ft. Worth, Texas: Church Starting Network, 2008. (www.churchstarting.net)

J.O. Terry, *Hope Stories from the Bible*. Ft. Worth, Texas: Church Starting Network, 2008. (www.churchstarting.net)

Daniel R. Sánchez and J.O. Terry. *LifeStory Encounters*. Ft. Worth, Texas: Church Starting Network, 2009. (www.churchstarting.net)

J. O. Terry, *Death Stories from the Bible*. Ft. Worth, Texas: Church Starting Network, 2009. (www.churchstarting.net)

J. O. Terry, *Food Stories from the Bible*. Ft. Worth, Texas: Church Starting Network, 2009. (www.churchstarting.net)

J. O. Terry, *Grief Stories from the Bible*. Ft. Worth, Texas: Church Starting Network, 2009. (www.churchstarting.net)

The Church Starting Network supplies all of these resources:

3515 Sycamore School Road, Fort Worth, Texas 76133

www.ChurchStarting.net

www.sembrariglesias.net

I was visiting the humble home of a farmer and his wife to share God's Word with some of the neighboring village people. Our team had arrived near evening. The couple insisted on feeding us. Next to their small thatch house was a building made of granite slabs standing on end as walls and others laid across the top for a roof. We were seated on straw mats inside. Soon the food was brought on plates made of mulberry leaves sewn together. The meal was a healthy portion of rice with a spoonful of ghee (clarified butter) on top. As I ate I was aware of munching sounds all around me. Then I noticed the stacks of baskets filled with mulberry leaves. Inside were hungry silkworms eagerly devouring their last meals. I was honored to be fed so graciously by this family and to dine with their little friends.

Contents

	Foreword	1
	Introduction to Food Stories	7
1.	God Provided Food for All His Creation	11
2.	God Provided Food for Adam and Eve	13
3.	Noah—Food for the Family and Animals	17
4.	Abraham—Food for Three Visitors	21
5.	Jacob and Esau—Birthright for a Bowl of Stew	25
6.	Jacob and Isaac—Meal of Deception for a Blessing	27
7.	Joseph—Famine and Forgiveness	31
8.	The Passover Meal—a Memorial	35
9.	A Craving—Meat and Manna	37
10.	The People Complained About Their Food	41
11.	Ruth—a Young Woman Who Gleaned in a Barley Field	43
12.	A Double Portion for Hannah	47
13.	A Table in the Presence of My Enemies	49
14.	Abigail's Wise Provision	51
15.	David—the King Who Shared His Food	55
16.	A Prophet Fed by Birds and a Meal Cooked by an Angel	57
17.	A Starving Widow's Last Meal	59

18.	Feeding the Enemy	61
19.	When Lepers Shared Their Food	63
20.	Hezekiah—the Great Passover Celebration	67
21.	Daniel and Friends Eat Wisely	69
22.	Jeremiah— A Starving Prophet	71
23.	When Jesus Fasted in the Desert	73
24.	Eating with Unwashed Hands	75
25.	Eating with Sinners at Matthew's House	77
26.	Hungering for Righteousness	79
27.	The Sinful Woman at Simon's Supper	81
28.	Lazarus—A Starving Beggar	83
29.	The Rich Fool	85
30.	A Starving Son Who Repented	87
31.	Food for the Hungry Multitude	91
32.	Jesus—the Bread Come Down from Heaven	93
33.	The Great Feast and Refused Invitations	95
34.	The Last Supper—Fellowship, Covenant and Betrayal	97
35.	Jesus—Do You Have Anything to Eat?	101
36.	Breakfast on the Beach	105
37.	The Believers Broke Bread Together	109
38.	Peter's Strange Dream	111
39.	Eating Food Offered to Idols	115
40.	Eating Worthily at the Lord's Table	117
41.	Meat or Milk?	119
42.	Full Bellies and Starving Souls	121
43.	Tree of Life Bearing Fruit for Life and Healing	123

44. A Place at the Table Saved for You......... 125
    Guidelines for Selecting Bible Stories......... 127
    Preparing the Bible Stories......... 131
    Considerations for Crafting (Oralizing)
    Bible Stories for Telling......... 133
    Telling the Stories......... 135
    Talking About & Teaching From Bible Stories... 141
    Getting Response and Drawing the Net......... 145
    Using Visuals to Tell Bible Stories......... 151
    References......... 153

FOREWORD

The Initial Idea

A number of years ago several of my colleagues among the media consultants for my mission board talked about the need for resource materials to use during disaster response and during various relief and development ministries. The need was to have some appropriate ministry resource materials already prepared and ready for distribution and immediate use. Time passed but the original concept of resource ministry materials was never developed. The recurring needs due to disasters and other ministries related to disaster response and relief efforts and clean water development projects did, however, continue unabated.

Awareness of Need

Because no materials specifically for disaster and relief needs existed, this storyer used suitable Bible stories that were already part of evangelism and training programs for rural and nonliterate people groups. Materials were not written so the stories used were those already known from frequent use. The stories were simply recalled when the ministry needs and opportunities arose.

Once, local Christians invited me to a city in India, where a severe earthquake had recently damaged many houses. I observed the need for stories of hope and encouragement rather than the typical evangelism set of stories. People needed to know there was a God who loved all people. Even when natural calamities occurred, He was powerful and able to provide help and bless people in their suffering and physical need.

The original awareness for materials to impress the ways of God to provide for human needs, planted years before, was at that time urgently reinforced. Further events finally led to action in beginning efforts to provide some of the ministry resources as thematic sets of Bible stories for specific ministry opportunities in the Asia-Pacific region where I was then serving.

Birth of the Water Stories

While working and visiting countries in the Asia-Pacific Region, I saw a need and opportunity to provide suitable Bible Storying resources to be used during clean-water projects in Bangladesh and later in Cambodia. While wells were being sunk and pumps cemented in, local village people came to stand around and watch the well teams at work. The teams completed a typical well project in a day or two. The work on the well provided an open opportunity to communicate with the people by appropriate Bible stories. The village people loved stories and the stories provided a form of entertainment related to the wells.

Later in Cambodia, I observed the *Water of Light* project that was providing locally manufactured sand filters with UV light sterilizers. Again, local people would come to watch the installation process. These gatherings provided another opportunity to tell the Bible stories. Other places, where various clean-water needs like dug wells and reservoirs existed, provided still more opportunities to share appropriate related water stories.

So *The Water Stories*[1] were gleaned from the Bible, covering many different aspects of water, its sources and uses and, finally, the "water of salvation." As the story sets spread from country to country, many reports arose from use of the story sets among thirsty peoples far and wide. The stories did not attempt to teach how to purify water, or what contaminated water, only to use the theme of water to teach spiritual truth leading to salvation.

The Water Stories could be used in conjunction with teaching about safe-water practices for family and community health.

Birth of the Grief Stories

About this same time another need became evident. I had used Bible stories that were selected initially for Muslim women, who were not interested in any "Christian" teaching, but who were attracted to stories about women who suffered misfortunes much like they experienced. The triggering idea came from reading a book telling how women in certain Central Asian countries gathered to tell their stories of misfortune and so to release their emotion among their peers.[2] The basic idea was interesting, but the women's stories lacked a good finish. So when the Bible stories about women's misfortunes were chosen, each was ended in a brief account about how God redeemed each woman's life. *The Grief Stories*[3] were provided without any attached teaching resources except for some helps for the storyer. The selected stories were found to provoke at times lively discussion among the women listeners leading to the opportunity for appropriate "Christian" teaching by the patient storyer to answer their questions and respond to their comments.

Birth of the Hope Stories

After leaving Asia for retirement, I was invited to teach Bible Storying at a training event in Bartlesville, Oklahoma. The Disaster Assistance Response Training (DART) conducted by Strategic World Impact[4] included personal health care for response teams while on mission, working among those of different cultures and world religions, and working with military and relief agency personnel. This training explained the need for using Bible Storying in a suitable ministry form to complement the physical relief ministry by providing a spiritual component.

Preparation for this first training time with DART led to compiling a set of stories especially chosen for use during disaster response ministry. *The Hope Stories* followed a general theme of the God who is Creator, who loves mankind whom He created, and is powerful to save, heal and help in times of disaster. Again, as in the other story sets, a subtle evangelistic theme runs through the stories, though the stories are generally developed to be pre-evangelistic. In many of the places where disaster response is needed, the local peoples are often resistant to traditional evangelistic witnessing, and sometimes openly hostile even during normal times. Stories are entertaining and engaging, and people will listen to them, to be heard without typical hostile response, even when they are not in full agreement with the story themes and outcome.

As it turned out only six months after *The Hope Stories* were prepared and shared digitally in the DART training, the disastrous tsunami occurred in Indonesia and surrounding countries. Immediately response teams began looking for spiritual ministry resources for use while there was opportunity and openness among the tsunami victims in Indonesia. Then not long afterward a massive earthquake in northeastern Pakistan again triggered a need for spiritual ministry resources to provide hope to distressed villagers.

Food Stories Needed

All three of the above sets of stories have been used to meet local ministry needs of both urgent relief and also longer-term development nature. At the time, I had wanted to do one story set on food. During the days of Bible Storying training among rural and tribal people of Bangladesh and one of the tribal groups in India, I noticed that among the stories of Jesus that were popular the Feeding of the Multitude story was almost always chosen to be retold by trainees.

There was joy among listeners as they heard the story of abundant food being provided through the miracle of Jesus. In addition, another story, the parable of the Great Banquet, really stirred up response. When the invited guests in the parable declined to come and eat after the food was prepared, the listeners' interest was aroused. In many cultures, to decline food that was prepared and served by the host was an unthinkable breach of etiquette.

Abundant food and eating together comprise a valued form of fellowship and satisfaction. A set of stories regarding food, therefore, should have a value during disaster response, relief ministries during famines, and on other occasions when the topic or theme of food is appropriate to garner attention, and initiate an ongoing opportunity to share more Bible stories leading to salvation of listeners, and initiate a subsequent church-planting movement.

A speaker I once heard at an urban ministry conference in Manila used an illustration to refer to appropriate teaching. He explained that people bring with them mental "baskets," large and small, into which they receive and carry away teaching they hear. Those with large baskets can receive much teaching, retain it, and take it with them. Those with small baskets can only retain and take away smaller amounts of teaching that is usually practical and relevant to their lives.

Efforts to continue providing teaching to those with smaller baskets results in overflow so that much is lost, or displaces what was heard first with what was heard later, resulting in only a small basketfull. And for others, whose baskets were "holey" or misshapen, or already filled with things from other sources (their prevalent religion, culture or beliefs), much of what was received went out through the holes, spilled due to the broken shape, or overflowed without displacing the old. And the speaker added that some who come with larger baskets go away disappointed because their baskets are not filled. The object, then, is to fit the teaching to the ability of the listeners to receive it and take it with them.

I recall the experiences of a mission volunteer who had come to the Philippines and was assigned to preach for five nights to people living in a mountainous area. The volunteer had preached a ten or fifteen minute message and sat down. The listeners looked puzzled. Finally an older man said to him: "Do you have any more to say? We have come a long way and the night is still early." So that volunteer preached what he had prepared for the second night. Still the people wanted more, until the volunteer was coaxed into sharing all that he had prepared for a whole week that one night.

The listeners were hungry to hear more good news. I have also experienced that old man's question: "Sir, is there not another story to tell?" So I warn those who go out to share Bible stories to be prepared to tell many stories to those whose hungry hearts long to be fed.

Another time I happened to arrive in India during a crisis that pitted Muslims against their Hindu neighbors. One man told me that their gods had failed them. We have a God who does not fail us. And we have the stories of our God's promises and provision for those whose gods have failed them.

We want to fill the baskets of spiritually hungry listeners while being mindful of the capacities of their baskets. For those who can receive more, we give more, and for those who can only receive little, we give what they can receive.

And we are ready to refill baskets as long as they keep coming for more.

You've heard the expression: Give a man a fish and he eats today. Teach him to fish and he can feed himself. So tell the stories today to feed their souls today. Teach the stories so the listeners can not only feed themselves spiritually day by day, but feed others in the days ahead, as well.

May the Lord provide the needed wisdom, insight, and anointing to tell effectively the stories of His providence during times of intense physical need and spiritual hunger.

J.O.Terry

INTRODUCTION TO FOOD STORIES

This set of stories—*The Food Stories*—is not exhaustive nor do I intend it to prescribe what you the storyteller must do. These stories are presented simply as a model of what you might tell, or to help you in selecting your own set of appropriate stories, and adapting (oralizing) them for telling appropriately among the people you will work with.

Normally I suggest that the stories not be translated from the wording I have used, but that you the storyteller develop the stories you will use from the Bible translation that you prefer using, or the local translation in the people's spoken language. As a storyteller I have taken some liberty in adapting the stories from a literate account to more of an oralized account suitable for sharing in an oral environment.

In addition, I have provided some pre-story suggestions (*Prepare the Food*) to use as well as some post-story comments and discussion questions (*Food for Thought*) to use as needed and where appropriate.

Some Bible stories refer to things that may become cultural problems for the people you seek to serve. Once a Hindu worshiper asked me if it were true that Christians "bite the cow." Typically the killing and eating of animals among vegetarian Buddhists can be offensive. Among Hindus, eating cattle can be a problem. In the story of Abraham's Three Visitors, or at the end of The Parable of the Prodigal Son, "killing the fatted calf" could cause some listeners to dislike the story. So general terms could be used like "preparing bread, meat, and curds" for the angels and preparing a "great feast" for the return of the lost son. These methods may keep the stories culturally acceptable. If these concerns are not a matter for your people, then disregard the suggestion.

In selecting appropriate stories to tell and adapting the stories for telling, the listeners' worldview should be considered. The insights from the local worldviews can inform story choices and how stories are adapted (crafted) for telling. At best this approach will help in contextualizing the stories or avoiding certain stories until a favorable time when the listeners are more likely to understand and be open to accept stories that vary with their beliefs and culture or their prejudices.

Using the Stories

The next section deals briefly with *Using the Stories* in typical response or relief ministry. Again, it is only suggestive. The Bible stories are presented chronologically, but you may find that another arrangement is better suited for local needs. The compilation of stories is a resource which means that you should pick and choose from among the stories which are better to tell and which fit into your ministry time among a people. Be prepared to repeat some of the stories as interest indicates. If by some reason you should tell all of the stories and still have opportunity, then by all means, feel free to repeat the series, or at least the more popular or most appropriate stories.

Ask the listeners which ones they would like to hear again. Review of previous (or the most recently told) stories gives the needed repetition, and may help to preserve connection of stories and themes. Generally, oral learners enjoy repetition as they hear again stories they already are familiar with, and even enjoy retelling the same stories themselves.

An alternative is to provide a recording of the stories that can be kept by the listeners and played over and over according to their interest. This could be via a cassette or digital player brought by the ministry team, and left with a responsible person to operate it.

Food Miracles Still Happen

Following is the story of a miraculous feeding. The story comes via colleagues working in a certain Southeastern Asia country that is sensitive regarding Christian ministry.

"We sat with some new believers over Christmas and listened to their stories. I never cease to be amazed at the workings of our God! Here is part of their story:"

"Since becoming followers of Jesus, we have a heart to share the gospel with all the Buddhists who live around us. We decided to host a holiday celebration and invite about 200 of our Buddhist friends to come. We are very poor, but we scraped together enough food to feed the estimated 200 who would attend. More than 600 came. We did not know what to do. We did not have nearly enough food to feed everyone. Even the Buddhist visitors began to comment about the small amount of food they saw and they were complaining.

I remembered the Bible story we had just learned how Jesus took a few fish and a few loaves of bread and fed more than 5,000 with them. We prayed that Jesus would multiply our small amount of food so that we could feed everyone.

Visitors lined up and we began to feed them. We fed all of them and had a great deal left over. We took what was left and went into the Buddhist villages, feeding the poor and homeless. When our visitors asked where the extra food came from, we told them Jesus had multiplied what little we had and made it a lot. They were all amazed and have been asking us many questions about Jesus ever since."

I can imagine that our Lord smiled as He observed that event. How He delights in answering the prayers uttered in simple faith. I found myself crying out, "Lord I believe, help thou my unbelief."

It is the local people who have made relief work possible in the aftermath of a big storm. It is they who have delivered food and aid and shared the Good News. The relief work has now extended to nearly 5,500 people! The Lord has provided blankets, rice, beans, oil, salt, sugar, candles, mosquito nets, water filters, soap, some clothing, and copies of the Word and letters of encouragement. For many, though they had little food, they were most excited about receiving the Word. They knew that though the food would be gone in a few weeks, their copy of the Word would feed their souls for years. Most people who previously had a copy lost it in the storm. Still, many others had never owned a copy of the Word. In most of the efforts to provide aid some people have come to believe in Jesus and fellowship groups are being started. (*name omitted for security*)

1. God Provided Food For All His Creation

Scripture Base: Genesis 1; Job 38:41; Psalm 107:9; 145:13b-16; Matthew 6:26

Prepare the Food:

Ask the listeners these questions and let them talk freely:
1. Where does your food come from? Who really provides it for you?
2. What part or role do listeners have in providing food for their own family?
3. Who helps listeners to grow their food?
4. What do listeners think might happen if God did not help them to grow, harvest, or catch the food they eat?

Serve the Meal:

God Provided Food for All His Creation

In the beginning God created the heavens and the earth. After the earth and heavens were created, then God created the plants and animals.

God said, "Let the land produce all kinds of seed-bearing plants and trees with fruit on them." And it was so. The land produced the plants and trees and God saw that it was good.

God said: "Let the water be filled with living creatures and let the birds fly through the skies." So God created the great creatures of the sea and every living thing that swims in the seas. And God made every kind of bird. God blessed the creatures and birds He had made and instructed them to increase in number.

Then God said, "Let the land produce living creatures according to their kinds: livestock, creatures that move along the ground, and wild animals." So God made the animals and saw that it was good.

"To all the beasts of the earth and all the birds of the air and all the creatures that move along the ground—everything that has the breath of life in it—I give every green plant for food." And it was so.

God asked a man named Job, "Who provides food for the raven when its young cry out to God and wander about for lack of food" (Job 38:41)?

Another prophet wrote about giving thanks to God for his unfailing love "...for He satisfies the thirsty and fills the hungry with good things. The Lord is....loving toward all He has made....the eyes of all look to God and You give them their food at the proper time" (Psa. 145:13b, 15).

The one called Jesus told his followers: "Look at the birds of the air; they do not sow or reap or store away in barns, and yet your heavenly Father feeds them" (Matt. 6:26).

We look to God our Creator to help provide our food.

Food for Thought:

1. Have the listeners heard this story before?
2. Do the listeners believe that God really helps us to have the food we need to eat?
3. What are some ways in which we have a part in providing our food?
4. Is there anything in the story the listeners would like to talk about?
5. Does this story remind us that God is faithful to provide food for His Creation?
6. Would anyone or the group like to retell this story?

Food for the Heart: "The eyes of all look to you, and you give them their food at the proper time. You open your hand and satisfy the desires of every living thing" (Psa. 145:15-16).

2. God Provided Food For Adam and Eve

Scripture Base: Genesis 1:26-29; 2:7-17, 20-22; 3:1-24

Prepare the Food:
1. Do listeners know what food the first man and woman ate?
2. Has anyone ever told listeners not to eat a certain food? What might happen if they did?
3. If listeners were warned not to eat a certain food, would they obey that warning?

Serve the Meal:

God Provided Food For Adam and Eve

God said, "Let us make man in our image, in our likeness." So God created them male and female. God blessed the man and woman and said for them to be fruitful and increase in number. Then God said, "I give you every seed-bearing plant on the face of the whole earth and every tree that has fruit with seed in it. These will be yours for food" (Gen. 1:29).

After God had formed the man out of the dust of the ground and breathed into him the breath of life, God placed the man in a garden God had planted. There were all kinds of trees growing there—trees that were pleasing to the eye, and trees that produce fruit that was good for food. In the middle of the garden were two special trees: the tree of life, and the tree of the knowledge of good and evil. God put the man in the garden to care for it.

Then God commanded the man, "You are free to eat from any tree in the garden; but you must not eat from the tree of the knowledge of good and evil. For when you eat of that tree, you will surely die."

After this God had caused the man to sleep and removed bone from his side and fashioned a woman and brought her to the man.

One day the serpent that was more clever than any of the wild animals said to the women: "Did God really say, 'You must not eat from any tree in the garden?'"

The woman replied, "We may eat fruit from the trees in the garden. But God did say, 'You must not eat fruit from the tree that is in the middle of the garden, and you must not touch it, or you will die.'"

"You will not surely die," the serpent replied. "God knows that when you eat of that tree your eyes will be opened and you will become wise like God, knowing good and evil."

When the woman saw that the fruit was pleasing to the eye, and good for food, and desirable for becoming wise, she took some and ate it. And she gave some to her husband, who was with her, and he ate it. Their eyes were opened, and they saw their nakedness, and became ashamed and hid themselves, and made coverings out of leaves.

God asked the man if he had eaten from the tree that God commanded him not to eat from. The man blamed the woman for giving him the fruit. The woman blamed the serpent that deceived her.

So God judged the disobedience of the serpent, the woman, and the man. To the man, Adam, God said, "Because you ate from the tree which I commanded not to eat from, the ground is now cursed and will produce thorns and thistles for you. Through painful work you will now grow your food. You will eat the plants of the field. By the sweat of your brow you will work until you die and return to the dust of the ground."

The man Adam named his wife Eve. God provided clothing of animal skins to cover their nakedness. Then God banished the man Adam and his wife Eve from the garden called Eden, and placed an angel with a flaming sword to guard the way to the tree of life so the man and woman could not eat from it and live forever because of their disobedience.

Food for Thought:
1. When God made the first man and woman, what food did He provide for them to eat?

2. When God placed the man Adam in the garden, what did God tell Adam about eating from the trees?
3. What warning did God give Adam about eating from a certain tree?
4. What did the woman Eve say when the serpent asked her if God said not to eat from any tree in the garden?
5. Who did the woman believe—God or the serpent?
6. Did the man Adam also eat the fruit from that tree?
7. What consequences did God pronounce because of the disobedience of Adam and Eve?
8. Now how would the man get food to eat?
9. After a life of hard work, what happens to the man?
10. If God made the world and all the plants and trees, who really helps man to have food to eat?

Food for the Heart: "If you fully obey the Lord your God and carefully follow all his commands...The Lord will open the heavens, the storehouse of his bounty, to send rain on your land in season and to bless all the work of your hands" (Deut. 28: 1a, 12a).

3. Noah—Food for the Family And Animals

Scripture Base: Genesis 6:5-22; 7:1-24; 8:1,15-21; 9:1-4, 12-13

Prepare the Food:

1. Ask listeners if they must at certain times of the year gather and store up food for their families and animals.
2. Have there been times during floods or cyclones when listeners' families and animals had little or no food to eat?
3. Here is a story about a righteous man who lived during a terrible flood when people and animals died. God told him what to do to save his family and the animals.

Serve the Meal:

Noah—Food for the Family And Animals

After the days of Adam and Eve, many years had passed and the population of the earth had increased. God saw how great mankind's wickedness on earth had become, and many hearts were filled with thoughts only of evil. God said, "I will destroy mankind—men, animals, creatures that move along the ground and birds. I am grieved that I have made them." But there was a man named Noah who found favor in God's eyes.

Noah was a righteous man who was blameless among the people of his day. He walked with God, that is, lived a life that was obedient and pleasing to God. So God revealed to Noah that He was going to put an end to all people because of their wickedness.

God then told Noah to prepare an ark or boat that was large enough to carry Noah's family and all the animals that God would bring to Noah to be saved. God said, "I am going to bring floodwaters on the earth to destroy all life. You are to bring into the ark two of all living creatures, male and female, to keep them alive. And you are also to bring seven pairs of all the clean animals and birds."

"You are also to take every kind of food that is to be eaten and store it away as food for your family and the animals."

Noah did everything God commanded him to do. At last when the ark and all the food was prepared, God told Noah to take his family and the animals into the ark and God closed the door. After seven days it began to rain. The rain continued for forty days and nights until the earth was flooded and everything with the breath of life in it perished. Noah and his family and animals were safe in the ark.

After many days had passed, God remembered Noah and all the wild animals and livestock with him in the ark, and sent a wind to dry up the waters. Then God said to Noah, "Come out of the ark, you and your wife, your three sons and their wives. Bring out every creature, animal and bird so they can be fruitful and replenish the earth."

Noah built an altar and sacrificed some of the clean animals and birds as a burnt offering. God was pleased and promised never again to curse the ground and destroy all living creatures.

God blessed Noah and his sons and said to them, "Be fruitful and increase in number and fill the earth. Now everything that lives and moves will be food for you. Just as I gave you the green plants for food, I now give you everything. But you must not eat meat that has its lifeblood still in it."

God placed a rainbow in the sky as a sign of his promise never to destroy the earth again by water.

Food for Thought:
1. Why did God want to destroy the people and animals during the time of this story?
2. Why did God look with favor on Noah?
3. What did God reveal to Noah that God was going to do?
4. What did God want Noah to do to save his family and the animals?
5. How would Noah's family and the animals have food to eat during this time?
6. Did Noah obey God?

7. After the flood, what did God tell Noah about the food he could eat?
8. What did God tell Noah that he must do before eating meat?
9. Is there anything in the story you don't understand or want to talk about?

Food for the Heart: "Everything that lives and moves will be food for you. Just as I gave you the green plants, I now give you everything" (Gen. 9:3).

4. Abraham—Food For Three Visitors

Scripture Base: Genesis 12:1-3; 17:1-6, 15-19; 18:1-14; 21:1-2

Prepare the Food:
1. Talk about the custom for feeding guests who visit the listeners?
2. What if some visitors arrived that listeners knew to be special or highly honored? What would they do?
3. Would listeners ask the visitors what is the purpose of their visit, or wait to see what the visitors had to say?

Serve the Meal:

Abraham—Food for Three Visitors

God said to a man named Abraham, "Leave your country, your people, and your father's household and go to a land I will show you. I will make you a great nation, and bless you." So Abraham left his land and his people and, with his wife Sarah, journeyed to the new land. But Abraham and his wife were now very old and his wife was childless.

Many years passed and still Abraham and his wife had no children. Abraham said to God, "What can you give me since I remain childless? You have given me no children."

God replied, "You will have a son of your own." Abraham believed God who counted Abraham righteous.

Years passed. Abraham bowed before God and asked: "Will a son be born to a man one hundred years old? Will my wife Sarah bear a child at ninety years age?"

God said, "Yes, your wife will bear a son and you will call him Isaac. I will establish my covenant with your son Isaac that Sarah will bear to you by this time next year."

One day while Abraham was sitting at the entrance to his tent he looked and saw three men standing nearby. When Abraham saw them, he hurried to meet them and bowed before them. Abraham said, "If I have found favor in your eyes, do not pass me by. I will bring some water so you can wash your feet and rest under this tree. Let me get you something to eat, so you can be refreshed and then you can go on your way."

"Very well," the men answered, "do as you say."

Abraham hurried to his wife Sarah and said, "Quick, take much fine flour and knead it and bake some bread." Then Abraham hurried to his herd of animals and selected a choice tender animal and gave it to his servant to prepare. Abraham then brought some curds and milk and the meat that had been prepared and set it before the three men. While the men ate, Abraham stood near them under the tree.

Soon one of the men spoke, "Where is your wife Sarah?

"She is in the tent," Abraham replied.

Then the man who was really an angel from God said, "I will surely return to you about this time next year, and Sarah your wife will have a son."

When Sarah heard these words she laughed to herself as she thought, "I am old and worn out, will I now have this pleasure?" The angel heard Sarah. "Why did you laugh?" the angel asked. "Is anything too difficult for God to do?"

So God was gracious to Sarah and did for her what He had promised. Sarah became with child and gave birth to a son at the very time God had promised. Abraham gave his son the name Isaac, a name that means laughter.

Food for Thought:

1. When God called Abraham to leave his country and people, did Abraham obey?
2. What did God promise to do for Abraham?
3. Did Abraham believe that God would keep his promise?
4. What did Abraham do when he saw the three visitors near his tent?
5. How did Abraham show hospitality to the three visitors?
6. What foods did Abraham ask his wife Sarah and his servant to prepare? Was it plentiful?

7. What is the custom of the listeners while visitors or their guests are eating? Do the listeners eat with them?
8. After the visitors had finished eating, what did the one called an angel of God say?
9. Did Sarah believe the words of the angel?
10. Did God keep his promise to provide a son for Abraham and Sarah?
11. What would the listeners do if an angel visited their home? What foods might they serve the visitors?

Food for the Heart: "Do not forget to entertain strangers, for by doing so some people have entertained angels without knowing it" (Heb. 13:2).

or

"Offer hospitality to one another without grumbling" (1 Pet. 4:9).

5. Jacob and Esau—Birthright For a Bowl of Stew

Scripture Base: Genesis 25:19-34; Hebrews 12:16-17

Prepare the Food:

1. Have any of the listeners ever longed for (coveted) what rightfully belonged to another?
2. Have any listeners given up what was rightfully theirs in order to satisfy a need like hunger?
3. Explain about the birthright that was the right of the older son to inherit a double portion from his father. It should be a valued right or possession not easily given away.
4. Here is a story about a brother who too easily gave away his birthright to fill his stomach with food.

Serve the Meal:

Jacob and Esau—Birthright For a Bowl of Stew

Abraham had a son named Isaac. After Isaac married a long time passed before his wife Rebekah became with child. When Isaac's wife finally became pregnant, she had two babies in her womb that began to struggle. God revealed to Rebekah that the two babies represented two different peoples and that the older would serve the younger.

When time came to give birth, there were twin boys in the womb. The first to come out was red and his body was like a hairy garment, so his parents named him Esau (*hairy*). After this, his brother came out, with his hand grasping his older brother's heel, so his parents named him Jacob *(one who grasps or deceives)*.

When the boys were grown, Esau became a skillful hunter, a man of the open fields who was the favorite of his father. Jacob was a quiet man who remained among the tents, the favorite of his mother.

Like Isaac, his father, Esau had a taste for wild game. Esau had gone hunting but had found nothing to kill. Jacob was cooking some lentil stew when Esau returned very hungry. Esau said to Jacob, "Quick, let me have some of that lentil stew! I am starving!"

But Jacob said, "First, sell me your birthright."

"Look, I am about to die," Esau said. "What good is a birthright to me?"

But Jacob said, "Swear to me first." So Esau swore an oath to his brother Jacob, selling him his birthright as the oldest son.

Then Jacob gave his brother Esau some bread and some lentil stew. Esau ate and drank, and then got up and departed.

So in that way Esau despised his birthright.

Food for Thought:

1. Who was the firstborn son? What was his right as the firstborn son?
2. Who was the hunter in the family? Who was cooking the lentil stew?
3. What did Esau want from his brother Jacob?
4. What did Jacob want from his brother Esau?
5. Did Esau agree to give Jacob his birthright?
6. What did Esau do after he swore to Jacob his birthright?
7. Do the listeners think that Esau did a good thing? Was Esau careless with an important inheritance?
8. Does Jacob's name (*grasper*) rightly describe him?

Food for the Heart: "See that no one is…godless like Esau, who for a single meal sold his inheritance rights as the oldest son. Afterward…when he wanted to inherit this blessing, he was rejected…though he sought the blessing with tears" (Heb. 12:16-17).

6. Jacob and Isaac—A Meal Of Deception for Blessing

Scripture Base: Genesis 27:1-47

Prepare the Food:

1. Have any of the listeners ever deceived anyone?
2. Would the listeners be willing to deceive their own father to gain something they wanted?
3. Here is the story of a mother who wanted her son to have his father's blessing. And to get it he must deceive his father. Here is the story of what happened.

Serve the Meal:

Jacob and Isaac—A Meal Of Deception for Blessing

When the father Isaac was old and his eyes weak so he could no longer see, he called for Esau his older son and said to him, "My son, I am now an old man and do not know the day of my death. Now then, get your bow and arrows and go out into the open country to hunt some wild game for me. Then prepare for me some tasty food I like so that I may eat and then give you my blessing before I die."

Rebekah, Isaac's wife, was listening as Isaac spoke to his son Esau. Rebekah then said to her favorite son Jacob, "Look, I overheard your father say to your brother Esau, 'Bring me some wild game and prepare for me some tasty food to eat, so that I may give you my blessing before I die.' Now, my son, listen carefully and do what I tell you: Go out to the flock and bring me two choice young goats, so I can prepare some tasty food for your father, just the way he likes it. Then take it to your father to eat, so that he may give you his blessing before he dies."

Jacob said to Rebekah his mother, "But my brother Esau is a hairy man, and I am a man with smooth skin. What if my father touches me? I would appear to be tricking him and would bring down a curse on myself rather than a blessing."

His mother Rebekah said to Jacob, "My son, let the curse fall on me. Just do as I say."

So Jacob brought the two choice young goats to his mother and she prepared some tasty food just the way his father Isaac liked it. Then Rebekah took the best clothes of Esau her oldest son and put them on her younger son Jacob. She also covered Jacob's hands and the smooth part of his neck with goatskins. Then Rebekah handed to her son Jacob the tasty food and bread she had made.

Jacob went to his father and said, "My father."

"Yes, my son," his father Isaac answered, "Who is it?"

"I am Esau your firstborn, I have done as you told me. Please sit up and eat some of my wild game so that you may give me your blessing."

Then Isaac asked his son, "How did you find the food so quickly, my son?"

"The Lord your God gave me success," Jacob replied.

Then Isaac said to Jacob, "Come near so I can touch you, my son, to know whether you really are my son Esau or not."

Jacob went close to his father Isaac who touched him. But then Isaac said, "The voice is the voice of Jacob, but the hands are the hands of Esau." So Isaac did not recognize Jacob for his hands felt hairy like those of his brother Esau. But Isaac asked again, "Are you really my son Esau?"

"I am," Jacob replied to his father.

Then Isaac said, "My son, bring me some of your wild game to eat, so that I may give you my blessing."

Jacob brought the tasty food to his father and he ate and drank. Then his father Isaac said to Jacob, Come here, my son, and kiss me."

So Jacob went close to his father and kissed him. When Isaac caught the smell of Esau's clothes, he blessed Jacob his younger son with the blessing intended for his son Esau.

After Isaac finished blessing Jacob, his brother Esau returned from hunting. He too prepared some tasty food and brought it to his father. "My father, sit up and eat some of my wild game, so that you may give me your blessing."

But Isaac said, "Who are you?"

"I am Esau, your firstborn son," he replied.

Isaac began to tremble and said, "Who is it then that hunted wild game and brought it to me? I ate it just before you came, and I blessed him."

When Esau heard his father's words he burst out with a loud and bitter cry and begged his father to bless him, too.

But Isaac said, "Your brother came deceitfully and took your blessing."

So Esau said, "Isn't he rightfully named Jacob? He has deceived me these two times, first taking my birthright and now he has taken my blessing." So Esau held a grudge against his brother Jacob and thought to kill Jacob after his father died.

But Jacob's mother Rebekah urged Jacob to leave home and flee to his uncle and remain there until Esau's anger ended. "When your brother is no longer angry with you and forgets what you did to him, I'll send word for you to return."

Food for Thought:

1. What did Isaac want his firstborn son to do for him? What did Isaac plan to do for his firstborn son?
2. What did Rebekah want Isaac to do for her favorite son?
3. Was Jacob willing to do what his mother said to do?
4. How did Rebekah dress Jacob in order to deceive his father?
5. Did Jacob's father think that he was Esau? What did Isaac keep asking Jacob?
6. How did Isaac test to see if Jacob were really his firstborn son?
7. After Isaac ate what he thought was the tasty wild game, did he bless Jacob?

8. What did Esau do when he returned with his wild game?
9. When Esau brought his food to Isaac his father, what did his father ask?
10. When Esau learned what happened, what did he ask his father to do for him?
11. What did Esau decide to do to Jacob?
12. What did Rebekah tell Jacob to do until Esau's anger ended?
13. If any of the listeners had been Jacob, would they have done what Jacob did?
14. If the listeners were Esau, how would they feel about what happened?
15. Did Jacob do the right and honorable thing or not?

Food for the Heart: "Trust in the Lord and do good.... Delight yourself in the Lord and he will give you the desires of your heart" (Psa. 37:3a, 4).

7. Joseph—Famine And Forgiveness

Scripture Base: Genesis 37:1-4, 12-28; 39:11-20; 40:1-23; 41:1-57; 42:1-25; 43:1-2, 24-34; 45:1-7; 47:11-25

Prepare the Food:

1. This is a rather lengthy story. The focus is to be kept mainly on those portions that relate to food with just enough of the other parts of the story to preserve the flow of the story.
2. There is a matter of God's provision through the work of Joseph to save the Egyptian people and Joseph's own family.
3. Talk (or ask) about how God might work through a person to provide food for people during their time of their need.

Serve the Meal:

Joseph—Famine and Forgiveness

There was a man who had twelve sons. His favorite son was named Joseph, the son of a different wife. Joseph's brothers were jealous of the favoritism shown by their father. So one time the father sent Joseph to see how his brothers were getting along with their flocks. When the brothers saw Joseph coming, they thought to kill him, but later decided to sell Joseph to some traders going to Egypt.

In Egypt Joseph was falsely accused by his master's wife and so was put into prison. There in prison were also two of the king's servants who had displeased the king. Each had dreams. One was the king's cupbearer who told his dream. Joseph interpreted it to mean that he would soon be released to serve the king again. The other man was a baker who in his dream had three baskets of bread on his head. But his dream meant that in three days he would be put to death.

Then the king of Egypt had two dreams. In one dream there were seven heads of healthy grain growing on a single stalk.

Then seven thin heads of grain sprouted and ate up the healthy grain. Again in a dream there were seven fat cows coming up from the river. But seven ugly lean cows ate up the fat ones. No one could interpret the dreams.

Someone, however, told the king that Joseph could interpret dreams. So Joseph was brought from prison and told the king's dreams. Joseph interpreted the dreams to mean that there would be seven years of great abundance of food followed by seven years of famine. The king was pleased with the interpretation and placed Joseph in charge of gathering food during the good years so there would be food enough during the famine years.

When the seven good years had ended there was famine just as Joseph said would happen. During the famine Joseph opened the storehouses and sold grain to the Egyptians. And all the countries around came to Egypt to buy food from Joseph.

A famine also arose in the land where Joseph's family lived. When Joseph's father learned there was grain in Egypt, he sent his remaining older sons to Egypt to buy food. Joseph recognized his brothers, but they did not recognize him. Joseph gave them grain but put their money back into one of the sacks. Later when their food was gone again the brothers had to return to Egypt to buy more grain. This time they brought their remaining younger brother with them. Joseph was overcome with emotion when he saw his younger brother. Joseph tested his older brothers to see if they were sorry for what they had done to Joseph who they said was dead.

Joseph invited his brothers to his house to eat a meal. He had the brothers seated according to their ages. The brothers wondered how this Egyptian could know their ages. Joseph himself was served apart from his brothers because it was detestable for Egyptians to eat with these foreigners. When the food was served to the brothers from Joseph's own table, the younger brother was given five times as much as anyone else. So the brothers ate and drank with Joseph.

It was later that Joseph revealed his identity to his brothers. They were fearful that Joseph might take revenge on them. But Joseph said, "I am your brother Joseph, the one you sold into slavery. And now do not be angry with yourselves for selling me here because God permitted it to save lives. God sent me ahead of you to provide food to save your lives. So it was not you who sent me here, but God." Then Joseph instructed his brothers to go bring his father and his brothers' families to live in Egypt where there was plenty of food.

All the people of Egypt came to Joseph to buy food. When the people's money was gone, the people said, "Give us food. Our money is gone. Why should we die?" So Joseph sold the people food in exchange for their livestock—their horses, sheep and goats, their cattle and donkeys. When their money and livestock were gone the people said, "Buy us and our land in exchange for food, and we will be in bondage to the king."

So Joseph bought the lands of the people and said, "Here is seed for you to plant. When the crops come in you must give the king a fifth of your crop." Joseph's family settled in Egypt and received lands to settle and they greatly increased in number. So Joseph saved his family and the Egyptians from the famine in their land.

Food for Thought:

1. Do listeners think that God knew about the famine about to happen?
2. How did God begin to use Joseph's life to prepare for the famine?
3. How did God reveal to the king of Egypt what was about to happen?
4. Was Joseph correct in his interpretation of the king's dream?
5. What did the king ask Joseph to do?
6. Why did Joseph's brothers go to Egypt?
7. Was Joseph kind to his brothers or revengeful?
8. Do the listeners have any custom where certain people do not eat together?

9. Did Joseph know why God sent him to Egypt? What did Joseph tell his brothers?
10. If any listeners had been Joseph, would they have been kind to their family even if the family mistreated them?
11. Do the listeners think that God could help them during time of famine?
12. If this story is being told during a famine relief effort, ask the listeners if God might be working through those who are providing the food.

Food for the Heart: "The eyes of all look to you, and you give them their food at the proper time" (Psa. 145:15).

or

"He provides food for those who fear him..." (Psa. 111:5).

8. The Passover Meal
A Memorial

Scripture Base: Exodus 12:1-30

Prepare the Food:

1. Do the listeners have any special feast days or times when people eat certain foods?
2. Are there any special rules or requirements about preparing the food and eating it?
3. How often is the feast or celebration celebrated? What is its significance to the individual? To the community?

Serve the Meal:

The Passover Meal—A Memorial

The descendants of Abraham had gone to live in Egypt during the days of Joseph and his family. They became a very great nation of people. But after Joseph died a new king came to rule that did not remember Joseph. And the new king feared that the descendants of Abraham, since they were not Egyptians, they might rebel and join with any foreign invaders. So the king made slaves of the people.

God heard the cries of the slaves and sent a man named Moses to deliver the people from Egypt. First Moses asked the king of Egypt to let the people go. When the king refused, then with God's help, Moses caused many disasters upon the land and people of Egypt. The last disaster was to be the death of all Egyptian first-born in each family.

But before this was to happen, God told Moses to instruct the people how to prepare. First each family was to kill a year-old male sheep or goat without any defect and place some of its blood on the sides and over the top of the door of their homes. This was to be a sign of protection for the family so that no one would die.

If the family were too small for a whole sheep or goat, they must share one with their nearest neighbor so there would be just enough food for each member of the family. The animals were to be killed just before evening. God warned the people, "Do not to eat the meat raw or cooked in water. It is to be roasted whole including head, legs, and inner parts over fire without breaking any of its bones. Do not leave any of the animals until morning. What remains uneaten must be burned." Also the people were to make bread without yeast and prepare bitter herbs to eat with the meat. The bitter herbs reminded the people of their bitter tears from suffering as slaves.

Then God instructed, "This is how you are to eat the meal. Eat it with your cloak tucked into your belt, standing with your sandals on your feet, and your walking staff in your hand. Eat the meal quickly; it is the Lord's Passover."

So the people obeyed the instructions about the blood and the Passover meal that night. No one died in any of the homes where the people obeyed God's instructions. For God had said that when He brought judgment on the king and the Egyptian people, the blood will be a sign for the people and God's angel would pass over that house.

Then God said, "This is a holy day you are to celebrate for generations to come as a festival to the Lord. For seven days you are to eat bread made without yeast. Celebrate this Feast of Unleavened Bread because it was on this day you were delivered from slavery in Egypt."

Food for Thought:
1. What instructions did God give the people about preparing their houses to prevent death of their first-born?
2. What instructions did God give about preparing the food to eat as a celebration of the Passover?
3. Did the people obey God? Is it important always to obey God?

Food for the Heart: "Therefore let us keep the Festival, not with the old yeast of malice and wickedness, but with bread without yeast, the bread of sincerity and truth" (1 Cor. 5:8).

What might these words mean?

9. A Craving — Meat And Manna

Scripture Base: Genesis 16:1-35; Numbers 11:3-33

Prepare the Food:

1. Talk about what foods listeners might crave when really hungry with nothing to eat.
2. Who or where do listeners turn when really hungry to satisfy hunger?
3. Do listeners think of others or only themselves when finding food?

Serve the Meal:

A Craving — Meat and Manna

After God delivered the descendants of Abraham out of the land of Egypt, the people had to travel across a desert to the land God was giving them. The food they had brought with them out of Egypt was now gone. The people were hungry. They said, "If only we had died by God's hand in Egypt! There we sat around pots of meat and ate all the food we wanted. Have we been brought out here to die?"

Then God said to Moses, "I will rain down bread from heaven for you. The people are to go out each day and gather just enough for that day. On the sixth day they are to gather enough for two days because there will be no bread on the seventh day."

Then Moses said, "You will know that it was God who gives you meat to eat in the evening and all the bread you want in the morning. He has heard your grumbling against him." Then Moses instructed all the people to gather before him.

God appeared in a bright cloud and said to Moses, "I have heard the grumbling of the people. Tell them, 'At evening you will eat meat. Then you will know that I am the Lord your God.'"

That evening quail came and covered the ground. And in the morning there was a layer of dew around the camp. When the dew was gone the ground was covered with thin flakes like frost. When the people saw it they said, "What is it?" So that is why it was called *manna*. It was white like coriander seed and tasted like wafers made with honey. Moses told the people to keep some of it in a jar as a reminder for the generations to come.

Another time later the people began to crave other food saying, "If only we had meat to eat! We remember the fish we ate in Egypt at no cost—also the cucumbers, melons, leeks, onions and garlic. Now we have lost our appetite. We never see anything but this manna!" Mosses heard the people of every family wailing, each at the entrance to their tent.

God became exceedingly angry and said to Moses, "Tell the people: 'Consecrate yourselves in preparation for tomorrow, when you will eat meat. God heard you when you wailed: If only we had meat to eat! We were better off in Egypt! Now God will give you meat, and you will eat it. You will not eat it for just one day, or two days, or five, ten or twenty days. But you will eat it for a whole month—until it comes out of your nostrils and you loathe it. You have rejected God saying: Why did we ever leave Egypt?'"

Moses said to God, "You say that you will give the people meat to eat for a whole month. Would the people have enough to eat if flocks and herds were slaughtered for them? Would they have enough if all the fish in the sea were caught for them?"

God answered Moses, "Is God's arm too short? You will now see whether or not what I say will come true for you."

Then a wind from God drove quail in from the sea. It brought the quail down all around the camp about three feet above the ground as far as a day's walk in every direction. All that day and night and the next day the people went out and gathered quail. While the people were eating the quail, while the meat was still between their teeth and could be swallowed, God's anger burned against the people and he struck them with a severe plague. Many died and were buried there because the people had craved other food.

Food for Thought:
1. When the people's food was gone, what did they do?
2. Did the people trust God to feed them, or were they thinking more of the former days as slaves in Egypt when they had plenty of food to eat?
3. Which is better to do when hungry: grumble or pray asking God for his help to provide food?
4. Was God pleased with the grumbling of the people?
5. Did God help the people anyway?
6. What did God provide for bread? Where did it come from?
7. What did God provide for meat?
8. Did the people learn a lesson at this time? Or did they soon forget and again begin to grumble?
9. Was God pleased with the people's grumbling? Or was he angry?
10. When Moses asked God where he would get enough meat to feet the people, what did God say? (Is God's arm too short?)
11. What did God tell Moses that he was going to do? For how long?
12. Did God keep his promise to provide meat?
13. When the people gathered quails all day and all night and again the next day, what did this say to God? (Perhaps it was saying: We don't trust you to feed us day-by-day. So we will gather enough to feed ourselves.)
14. Because of the craving of the people, what happened to them?
15. What if the listeners were among those people. What would they have done? Would they trust God to feed them day-by-day? Or would they also want to do like the people and gather more than they needed for each day?

16. Do the listeners believe that God is powerful (That his arm is not too short) to feed them?
17. What should people do when they need food? Grumble (complain) or have faith in God to help them?
18. What might God ask of the people in return? (Their faith in him as the only true God. Their trust in him to provide for their needs.)
19. What other needs might people have and should turn to God to ask and receive?
20. We will see in the stories that God wants our obedience when He tells us what to do, and our faith and trust in Him at all times including our times of need.

Food for the Heart: "The people asked, and God brought them quail and satisfied them with the bread of heaven" (Psa. 105:40).

10. The People Complained About Their Food

Scripture Base: Numbers 21:4-9; Psalm 78: 17-19, 20b, 22-29

Prepare the Food:

1. This is another story about a time when the people again complained about the food they were eating. Talk about some reasons why people might complain about the food they are given to eat.
2. When unhappy people complain, whom do they complain against or hold responsible?
3. What if there were serious consequences for complaining, would listeners still do it?

Serve the Meal:

The People Complained About Their Food

Abraham's descendants continued on their journey from Egypt to the land that God had promised to give them. But the people grew impatient along the way. They began to speak against God and against Moses their leader. The people said, "Why have you brought us out of Egypt to die in the desert? There is no bread! There is no water! And we detest this miserable food!"

Then God sent poisonous snakes among the people. The snakes bit the people and many became sick and died. The people came to Moses and said, "We sinned when we spoke against God and against you. Pray to God so he will take away the poisonous snakes from us." So Moses prayed for the people.

God said to Moses, "Make a snake of bronze and put it up on a pole so that anyone who is bitten by a poisonous snake can look at it and live."

So Moses made a bronze snake and put it up on a pole. Then when anyone was bitten by a snake and looked at the bronze snake on the pole, they lived.

Many years later, one of the people's prophets wrote about this time when the people complained about their food. He wrote:

> The people continued to sin against him, rebelling in the desert against the Most High. They willfully put God to the test by demanding the food they craved. They spoke against God, saying, 'Can God spread a table in the desert? Can he also give us food? Can he supply meat for his people?...For they did not believe in God or trust his deliverance. Yet he gave a command to the skies above and opened the doors of the heavens; he rained down manna for the people to eat, he gave them the grain of heaven. Men ate the bread of angels; he sent them all the food they could eat...He rained down meat on them like dust...They ate until they had more than enough, for he had given them what they craved (Psa. 78: 17-29).

Food for Thought:

1. Did God know the people were hungry?
2. Had God been providing food for the people to eat?
3. Did the people like the food that God provided?
4. Did the people show a lack of respect and thankfulness to God for what He provided?
5. God counted the people's complaining as sin, and God judged their sin and sent punishment.
6. But God is also a God of mercy for He also provided a way for those who sinned and were about to die to be healed and live.
7. When we are hungry, who should we turn to for food? When we receive His food what should we give in return?

Food for the Heart: "And my God will meet all your needs according to his glorious riches in Christ Jesus" (Phil. 4:19).

11. Ruth—A Young Woman Who Gleaned in a Barley Field

Scripture Base: Ruth: 1-4

Prepare the Food:

1. This is a sad story with a happy ending. The story begins with a famine and moves on to a time of plenty and great blessing.
2. Ask the listeners if they believe that God can redeem (overcome) any misfortune in their lives.
3. Ask: Could it be that sometimes God permits things to happen that will lead to greater blessing if we are faithful and trust Him?

Serve the Meal:

Ruth—A Young Woman Who Gleaned in a Barley Field

There was a man named Elimelech whose wife was named Naomi. They had two unmarried sons. There came a famine in their land so the family went to a neighboring country to live for a while. In this new country the two sons each married a local girl. In time the husband Elimelech and the two sons each died leaving Naomi a widow and the two daughters-in-law also as widows.

When Naomi heard that God had come to the aid of her people by providing food for them, Naomi and her two daughters-in-law prepared to return to Naomi's homeland. But Naomi urged her two daughters-in-law each to return to their own people. But one named Ruth replied, "Don't urge me to leave you or to turn back from you. Where you go I will go, and where you stay I will stay. Your people will be my people and your God will be my God. Where you die, I will die, and there I will be buried." When Naomi realized that Ruth was determined to go with her, she stopped urging Ruth.

So the two women returned to Naomi's homeland. They arrived at the beginning of the barley harvest. Naomi had a relative on her husband's side of the family. Ruth said to

Naomi, "Let me go to the fields and pick up the leftover grain behind anyone in whose eyes I find favor." So Ruth went and began to glean in the fields behind the harvesters.

As it turned out Ruth was working in the field belonging to the relative of Naomi's husband. When the relative, Boaz, arrived he asked the harvesters, "Whose young woman is that?" The harvesters replied, "She is the one who came back with Naomi and asked, 'Please let me glean and gather among the sheaves left behind by the harvesters.' She went into the field and has worked steadily from morning until now, except for a short rest in the shelter."

So Boaz said to Ruth, "My daughter, listen to me. Don't go and glean in another field, and don't go away from here. Stay here with my servant girls. Watch the field where the men are harvesting, and follow along after the girls. I have told the men not to touch you. And whenever you are thirsty, go and get a drink from the water jars." Ruth bowed down with her face to the ground.

At mealtime Boaz said to Ruth, "Come over here. Have some bread and dip it in the vinegar." When Ruth sat down among the harvesters, Boaz offered Ruth some roasted grain. She ate all she wanted and had some left over. Then Ruth got up to go glean. Boaz gave orders to his men, "Even if she gathers among the sheaves, don't embarrass her. Rather, pull out some stalks for her from among the bundles and leave them for Ruth to pick up."

So Ruth gleaned until evening. Then Ruth threshed the barley she had gathered. She carried it back to town, and Naomi saw how much Ruth had gathered. Ruth also brought with her what she had left over after she had eaten enough.

Naomi asked Ruth where she went to glean. When Ruth told her, Naomi said, "Blessed be the man who took care of you. That man is a close relative." Ruth also said that Boaz told her to stay with his workers until they finished harvesting all Boaz' grain.

Naomi was concerned about finding a home for Ruth, someone to provide for her. So Naomi told Ruth to bathe and prepare herself, and then go to the threshing floor where Boaz and the men would be spending the night. After everyone has eaten and drank and lay down to sleep, to go and lie at the feet of Boaz. Ruth did as Naomi told her. When Boaz woke during the night he discovered Ruth and asked, "Who are you?" Ruth said, "I am your servant Ruth." Boaz was pleased that Ruth had chosen him over the younger men. So he said, "Stay here until morning." Ruth lay at Boaz' feet until morning, but got up quietly before anyone would recognize her. Then Boaz said, "Bring me the shawl you are wearing and hold it out." Boaz poured out six measures of barley for Ruth and then sent her back to town.

Later Boaz went to town and spoke to a nearer relative and asked if he would be willing to redeem the land belonging to Naomi's dead husband. When the relative declined, then Boaz redeemed it, buying the land from Naomi. Boaz then took Ruth to be his wife. God enabled Ruth to conceive and she gave birth to a son. The friends of Naomi rejoiced with her because Ruth her daughter-in-law who was better than seven sons had given birth to a son. Naomi took the child and laid him in her lap and cared for him.

Food for Thought:

1. What caused Naomi and her husband and sons to leave their homeland?
2. After they had lived in the neighboring land for a time, what happened to the three men?
3. What did Ruth say to Naomi when Ruth wanted to go with Naomi?
4. Where did Ruth go to glean? Do you think this was by accident or chance, or was God directing Ruth to the best place for food?
5. How did Boaz show his kindness toward Ruth as she gleaned in his fields?
6. How was Ruth generous toward Naomi when she returned home? (Shared her remaining roasted grain from her meal.)
7. What was Naomi's plan for Ruth to do on the night of threshing?
8. As a result of Ruth's sleeping near Boaz, what did he go to do when morning came?

9. How did God bless Ruth? (Gave her a generous and kind husband and a son.)
10. List the ways in which God provided food for Naomi and Ruth. Do the listeners think that Ruth learned to trust God to provide for her needs?

Food for the Heart: "Therefore I tell you, do not worry about your life, what you will eat or drink; or about your body, what you will wear. Is not life more important than food, and the body more important than clothes? Look at the birds of the air; they do not sow or reap or store away in barns, and yet your Heavenly Father feeds them. Are you not much more valuable than they?" (Matt. 6:25-26).

12. A Double Portion for Hannah

Scripture Base: Leviticus 7:11-21; 1 Samuel 1:1-28

Prepare the Food:

1. Read Leviticus 7:11-21 about the fellowship offering. Note verse 15 about eating the meat. Explain about this shared offering with the listeners.
2. Are any of the women among the listeners barren? Is this a problem for a woman in their society? Would their husband still love them?
3. This story begins at the time and place of the annual fellowship offering and worship.

Serve the Meal:

A Double Portion for Hannah

A man named Elkanah had two wives. One, named Hannah, was barren. The other, named Peninnah, had children. Year after year this man went from his town to worship and sacrifice before Lord God Almighty at the temple.

Whenever the day came for Elkanah to sacrifice, he would give portions of the meat to his wife Peninnah and to all her sons and daughters. But to Hannah he gave a double portion because Elkanah loved Hannah even though God had closed her womb.

And because God had closed Hannah's womb, Peninnah kept provoking Hannah in order to irritate her. This went on year after year. Whenever Hannah went up to the temple to worship, Peninnah kept provoking her until Hannah wept and would not eat. Elkanah would say to Hannah, "Why are you weeping? Why don't you eat? Why are you downhearted? Don't I mean more to you than ten sons?"

Once when they had finished eating and drinking after the sacrifice, Hannah stood up. The priest for the holy place was sitting on a chair by the doorpost of the temple. In bitterness of soul Hannah wept much and prayed to God. And she made a vow saying, "Oh Lord God Almighty, if you will look upon my misery and give me a son, I will give him to you for all the days of his life."

As Hannah kept praying, the priest watched her mouth. Hannah was praying in her heart, and her lips were moving but her voice was not heard. The priest thought Hannah was drunk. So the priest said to Hannah, "How long will you keep on getting drunk? Get rid of your wine."

Hannah replied, "I am a woman who is deeply troubled. I have not been drinking wine. I am pouring out my soul to God. Do not take me for a wicked woman. I am praying out of my anguish and grief."

The priest said, "Go in peace. And may God grant you what you have asked." So Hannah was comforted and went her way and ate her food. Her face was no longer downcast.

After Elkanah and his wives returned home, he lay with his wife Hannah and she conceived and gave birth to a son. When it was again time for the sacrifice, Hannah said she would stay with her son until he was weaned and then would go to present him before God. When the boy was older Hannah brought him to the temple along with a bull for sacrifice, some flour and a skin of wine. Hannah said to the priest, "I am the woman who stood beside you praying for a child. Now I am here to present him to God."

Food for Thought:

1. Why wouldn't Hannah eat?
2. How did her husband show his kindness to Hannah?
3. What did Hannah ask God to give her? After her prayer did Hannah eat? Did this show she trusted God to help her?
4. Did God answer Hannah's prayer?

Food for the Heart: "The Lord is good to all; he has compassion on all he has made" (Psa. 145:9).

13. A Table in the Presence Of My Enemies

Scripture Base: Psalm 23

Prepare the Food:

1. Is it safe to eat while surrounded by enemies?
2. Who could protect someone so they could eat and live in safety?
3. Do any of the listeners feel they are surrounded or threatened by enemies?

Serve the Meal:

A Table in the Presence Of My Enemies

One of the kings who ruled over the descendants of Abraham was named David. In his early years David was a shepherd. When the prophet went to anoint a new king he asked David's father, "Are these all the sons you have?"

David's father replied, "There is still the youngest. But he is tending the sheep." That son was David.

One time when David left his flock of sheep and was facing a giant he said, "Your servant has been keeping his father's sheep. When a lion or bear came and carried off a sheep from the flock, I went after it, struck it and rescued the sheep from its mouth." So from a shepherd's heart David wrote this psalm (song) of praise and trust in God.

> The LORD is my shepherd, I shall not be in want.
>
> He makes me lie down in green pastures, he leads me beside quiet waters,
>
> He restores my soul. He guides me in paths of righteousness for his name's sake.
>
> Even though I walk through the valley of the shadow of death, I will fear no evil, for you are with me; your rod and your staff, they comfort me.

You prepare a table before me in the presence of my enemies. You anoint my head with oil; my cup overflows.

Surely goodness and love will follow me all the days of my life, and I will dwell in the house of the LORD forever.

Another writer said these words: "Then we your people, the sheep of your pasture, will praise you forever; from generation to generation (Psa. 79:13).

Food for Thought:

1. What kind of shepherd was David—good or bad?
2. What did David do for his flock? (guarded them and rescued them from danger)
3. Do the listeners find comfort in the words of this psalm?
4. Talk about how God might spread a table in the presence of one's enemies.
5. Does this psalm mean that listeners can trust God to protect as well as to provide for their needs in any circumstance?
6. If God will do these things for the listeners, will they be willing to trust God for his help and care and to always praise God from generation to generation?

Food for the Heart: "How great is your goodness, which you have stored up for those who fear you, which you bestow in the sight of men on those who take refuge in you" (Psa. 31:19).

14. Abigail's Wise Provision

Scripture Base: 1 Samuel 25:1-42

Prepare the Table:
1. Do any of the listeners know a very wealthy person?
2. Is that person generous or selfish about sharing with others?
3. Do listeners know anyone with a generous spirit who might intercede with such a wealthy person to share with those in need or who had helped him in some way?

Serve the Meal:

Abigail's Wise Provision

There was a certain man named Nabal who was very wealthy. Nabal possessed large flocks of sheep and goats. Nabal's wife Abigail was a very intelligent and beautiful woman. But Nabal was stingy and mean in his dealings.

When David heard that Nabal was shearing his sheep, David sent ten young men to Nabal to greet him in David's name. The messengers were to remind Nabal that David and his men did not mistreat any of Nabal's shepherds, and the whole time while David and his men were near by, nothing of Nabal's was missing. Since it was festive time, David asked if Nabal could share some food for his men.

But Nabal answered, "Who is this David? Why should I take my bread and water, and the meat I have slaughtered for my shearers, and give it to David's men?"

So David's men went back and reported what Nabal said. David became angry and said to his men, "Put on your swords!"

One of Nabal's servants told his wife Abigail that David sent messengers to greet his master but instead his master insulted the messengers and David. The servant reminded Abigail that night and day David and his men had protected those herding Nabal's sheep. Then the servant said, "Nabal is such a wicked man that no one can talk with him.'"

Abigail lost no time. Quickly she gathered two hundred loaves of bread, two skins of drink, five slaughtered sheep, a large quantity of roasted grain, cakes of raisins and pressed figs, and loaded the food on donkeys. Abigail sent the servants ahead with the food, and she followed but did not tell her husband Nabal.

Abigail met David just as he was saying how useless it was to watch over Nabal's flocks and how Nabal had insulted him. When Abigail saw David, she quickly got off her donkey and bowed down with her face to the ground. She fell at David's feet and begged David not to pay any attention to wicked Nabal. She said his name is "Fool" and folly goes with him. Then Abigail said, "Please forgive the offence and let this gift of food be given to the men who follow you."

David said to Abigail, "Praise be to God who has sent you today to meet me. May you be blessed for your good judgment and for keeping me from bloodshed in avenging Nabal."

Then David accepted from Abigail's hand what she had brought to him and said, "Go home in peace. I have heard your words and granted your request."

When Abigail returned to Nabal, he was holding a feast like that of a king. Nabal had been drinking and was very drunk, so Abigail told Nabal nothing until the next day. Then in the morning Abigail told Nabal all these things, and his heart failed him and Nabal became like a stone, and died ten days later.

When David heard that Nabal had died, he sent word to Abigail asking her to become his wife. Abigail said, "Here is your maidservant, ready to serve you and wash the feet of my master's servants." So Abigail became David's wife.

Food for Thought:

1. Talk about why such a wealthy man could be so stingy?
2. Talk about how different Abigail was.
3. How did Nabal show his selfishness?
4. How did Abigail demonstrate her generous spirit?

5. What happened to Nabal when he learned what his wife had done?
6. Talk about Abigail's prevention of bloodshed as David intended to take revenge on Nabal for his insults and selfishness.
7. What words did David say to Abigail when she gave the food to David for his men?
8. Who was wiser: Nabal or Abigail?
9. Was Nabal judged for his selfishness?
10. Would the listeners rather be a Nabal or an Abigail?
11. God who created the world we live in has been very generous to all people. God watches over all just as David and his men watched over Nabal's flocks. What should be our attitude toward God: Like that of Nabal or like that of Abigail? In a later story we will see what God has done for us. And we will have time to consider what we might do in return for God.

Food for the Heart: "Command those who are rich in this present world not to be arrogant nor to put their hope in wealth, which is so uncertain, but to put their hope in God, who richly provides us with everything for our enjoyment. Command them to do good, to be rich in good deeds, and to be generous and willing to share" (1 Tim. 6:17-18).

15. David—the King Who Shared His Food

Scripture Base: 2 Samuel 9:1-13

Prepare the Table:

1. Do listeners know of anyone they would like to show kindness to?
2. Would they be willing for that person to eat at their table as one of their own family?
3. Would it make any difference if that person were crippled?

Serve the Meal:

David—The King Who Shared His Food

After David became king he asked, "Is there anyone still left of the house of King Saul to whom I can show kindness for the sake of Jonathan?" For Jonathan was Saul's son and David's close friend.

There was a servant of King Saul's household. David asked him, "Is there one still left of the house of Saul to whom I can show God's kindness?"

The servant replied, "There is still a son of Jonathan; he is crippled in both his feet."

So King David had crippled Mephibosheth brought to him. When Mephibosheth arrived he bowed down to pay honor to David. David said to him, "Mephibosheth!" And he replied, "I am your servant."

David said, "Don't be afraid for I will surely show you kindness for the sake of your father Jonathan. I will restore to you all the land that belonged to your grandfather Saul, and you will always eat at my table."

Mephibosheth bowed down and said, "What is your servant that you should notice a dead dog like me?"

Then King David called for Saul's servant and said, "I have given to your master's grandson everything that belonged to

King Saul and his family. You and your sons are to farm the land for him and bring in the crops, so that your master's grandson can be provided for. And Mephibosheth, grandson of your master, will always eat at my table."

Then the servant said to King David, "Your servant will do whatever the king commands his servant to do." So Mephibosheth ate at David's table like one of King David's own sons.

Food for Thought:

1. Why did King David want to show kindness to anyone of King Saul's family?
2. Who did the servant say still remained?
3. His name is difficult to pronounce. The meaning of the name is "one who struggles against shame." He was five years old when his father and grandfather were killed in a battle. While escaping, his nurse picked him up to flee, but as she hurried to leave, Mephibosheth fell and became crippled in both feet (2 Samuel 4:4). He was also called Merib-Baal (1 Chronicles 8:34) which means "idol-breaker." His name may have been changed because Baal was associated with idol worship.
4. How did Mephibosheth show his humility before David?
5. How did David show his kindness and generosity toward Mephibosheth?
6. Did Mephibosheth do anything to earn David's kindness?
7. How does God show kindness toward us?
8. Must we earn God's kindness or does he give it freely because He loves and cares for us?

Food for the Heart: "A generous man will prosper; he who refreshes others will himself be refreshed" (Prov. 11:25).

16. A Prophet Fed by Birds and A Meal Cooked by an Angel

Scripture Base: 1 Kings 16:30-31, 33; 17:1-6;19:1-18

Prepare the Table:

1. Would listeners be willing to eat food brought to them by birds?
2. What if an angel cooked food for the listeners to eat?
3. Here is the story of a prophet of God who was fed in these unusual ways while obeying God.

Serve the Meal:

A Prophet Fed by Birds And A Meal Cooked by an Angel

It happened during the days of King Ahab who did more evil in the eyes of God than all the other kings before him. He not only committed sins and thought nothing about it, but he married a foreign woman who came and brought her religion of false prophets. King Ahab provoked the Lord God to anger because of his evil ways.

So God sent a prophet named Elijah to proclaim: "As the Lord, the God of Abraham's people lives, whom I serve, there will be neither dew nor rain in the next few years except at my word."

Then God's word came to Prophet Elijah saying, "Leave here and hide in a ravine east of the river. You will drink from the brook, and I have ordered ravens to feed you there."

Prophet Elijah did what God commanded. He went to that ravine where a brook flowed and stayed there. The ravens brought him bread and meat in the morning and bread and meat in the evening, and he drank from the brook.

Sometime later after Prophet Elijah had offered a sacrifice on a mountain to the true God and had all the false prophets put to death, King Ahab told his wife. So the wife of King Ahab sent word that she would have Prophet Elijah prophet killed.

Prophet Elijah was afraid and ran for his life. He left his servant behind and went a day's journey into the desert. At last Prophet Elijah came to a small tree and sat down under it and prayed that he might die. He said, "I have had enough, Lord. Take my life; I am no better than my ancestors." Then Prophet Elijah lay down under the tree and fell asleep.

All at once an angel touched him and said, "Get up and eat." Prophet Elijah looked around, and there by his head was a cake of bread baked over hot coals, and a jar of water. He ate and drank and then lay down again.

The angel of the Lord came back a second time and touched him and said, "Get up and eat, for the journey is too much for you." So Prophet Elijah got up and ate and drank. He was strengthened by that food so that he could travel forty days and forty nights until he reached the mountain of God.

At a cave God spoke to Prophet Elijah and encouraged him to go back. You are to anoint a new king over the people. God reminded Prophet Elijah that there were seven thousand men who had not bowed down to worship the false god Baal and all whose mouths had not kissed the false god.

Food for Thought:
1. Who was really providing food for Prophet Elijah to eat?
2. Do listeners consider ravens clean or unclean birds?
3. When did the birds bring food for the prophet to eat?
4. Why do listeners think God sent an angel to feed Prophet Elijah?
5. Why did the angel tell the prophet to eat again?
6. Is God able to provide our food when we need it?
7. Would listeners accept what God provided to eat?

Food for the Heart: "Let us give thanks to the Lord for his unfailing love and his wonderful deeds for men, for he satisfies the thirsty and fills the hungry with good things" (Psa. 107:8-9).

17. A Starving Widow's Last Meal

Scripture Base: 1 Kings 17:7-16

Prepare the Table:
1. Would listeners share their last food with a stranger who asked?
2. Have listeners at one time or another run out of food for their families?
3. Would listeners trust someone who told them what to do in order to have abundant food?

Serve the Meal:

A Starving Widow's Last Meal

After Prophet Elijah was fed by ravens and drank from the brook, the drought continued. At last the brook dried up because there was no rain. Then God sent word to Prophet Elijah: "Go at once to a certain town and stay there. I have commanded a widow in that place to supply you with food." So Prophet Elijah obeyed God and went to that town. When he arrived at the town gate, a widow was there gathering sticks.

Prophet Elijah called to the widow and asked, "Would you bring me a little water in a jar so I may have a drink?" As the widow was going to get the water, the prophet called out, "And please bring me a piece of bread."

The widow replied, "As surely as the Lord your God lives I don't have any bread. I only have a handful of flour in a jar and a little oil in a jug. I am gathering a few sticks to take home and make a meal for myself and my son, that we may eat it and then die."

Prophet Elijah said to the widow, "Don't be afraid. Go home and do as you have said. But first make a small cake of bread for me from what you have and bring it to me. Then make something for yourself and your son. For this is what the Lord God says: 'The jar of flour will not be used up and the jug of oil will not run dry until the day the Lord gives rain on the land.'"

So the widow went away and did as Prophet Elijah had told her. So there was food every day for Prophet Elijah and for the woman and for her family. The jar of flour was not used up and the jug of oil did not run dry, in keeping with the word of God spoken through Prophet Elijah.

Later the widow said, "Now I know that you are a man of God and that the word of God from your mouth is the truth."

Food for Thought:

1. Did God already have a plan for feeding Prophet Elijah when the brook dried up?
2. What do listeners think about Prophet Elijah asking for the widow's last food?
3. Did the widow obey Prophet Elijah?
4. What happened after the widow baked bread for Prophet Elijah?
5. How long did the flour and oil last?
6. Did Prophet Elijah obey the words of God?
7. Did the widow obey the words of God spoken through Prophet Elijah?
8. If listeners had been the widow, would they have obeyed the words spoken by the prophet?
9. What might have happened if the widow had not obeyed?
10. Do listeners think that God knew the widow would obey?
11. Can we say that if we expect a blessing, then we must obey what God says to do?

Food for the Heart: "He provides food for those who fear him..." (Psa. 111:5).

18. Feeding the Enemy

Scripture Base: 2 Kings 6:8-23

Prepare the Food:
1. How would listeners treat their enemy if the enemy were captured without any fighting?
2. What would be a kind thing to do for one's enemy?
3. Have any listeners done kind things for their enemies?

Serve the Meal:

Feeding the Enemy

A foreign king was at war with the descendants of Abraham. After talking with his officers he said, "I will set up my camp in such and such a place." The Prophet Elisha sent word to the king of Abraham's people warning him to beware of the plans of the enemy. Time and time again Prophet Elisha warned the king in this way.

The foreign king was very angry and called for his officers and asked which one of them was betraying his plans. They replied that none of them was the guilty person. It was because of the Prophet Elisha who tells his king every thing spoken in the king's bedroom!

So the foreign king ordered his officers to find Prophet Elisha and capture him. A report came back telling where Prophet Elisha was staying. The foreign king sent horses and chariots and surrounded the city. When Prophet Elisha rose the next morning the army had surrounded the city. "Oh my, what shall we do?" Prophet Elisha's servant asked.

"Don't be afraid. Those who are with us are more than those who are with them," the prophet replied. Then Prophet Elisha prayed, "O Lord, open my servant's eyes so that he may see." Then the Lord opened the servant's eyes, and he looked and saw the hills full of horses and chariots of fire all around Prophet Elisha.

As the enemy army came toward him, Prophet Elisha prayed to God, "Strike these people with blindness." So the enemy army became blind.

Then Prophet Elisha told the blinded men, "This is not the road and this is not the city. Follow me, and I will lead you to the man you are looking for." So the prophet led the blind army to the city where his king lived. After they entered the city, Prophet Elisha prayed again, "Lord, open the eyes of these men so they can see." Then the Lord opened their eyes and they looked, and there they were, inside the city of Abraham's people.

When the king saw the enemy army he asked, "Shall I kill them, my father? Shall I kill them?"

Prophet Elisha answered, "Do not kill them. Would you kill men you have captured with your own sword? No, instead set food and water before them so they may eat and drink and then go back to their master."

So the king prepared a great feast for the foreign army. And after they had finished eating and drinking, he sent them away, and they returned to their master, the foreign king.

Food for Thought:

1. Was Prophet Elisha afraid when he saw the enemy army that surrounded him?
2. What did the prophet mean when he said, "Those who are with us are more than those who are with them?"
3. Did God answer Prophet's Elisha prayers to first blind the men and then to open their eyes?
4. What did the king want to do to the captured army?
5. What did Prophet Elisha tell the king to do?
6. Later we will hear the teaching about how to do good to those who hate us and are our enemy.

Food to Take Away: "If your enemy is hungry, give him food to eat; if he is thirsty, give him water to drink" (Psa. 25:21).

19. When Lepers Shared Their Food

Scripture Base: 2 Kings 6:24-7:20

Prepare the Food:

1. Ask the listeners if they have experienced a time of famine when there was little or no food to eat?
2. Ask what they did (or might do) to find food to eat during a famine?
3. If by chance someone found food, would they eat it or hide it, or go tell others the good news?

Serve the Meal:

When Lepers Shared Their Food

A time came when a foreign army surrounded the city of Samaria. There was a great famine in the city. The siege lasted so long that a donkey's head for food was very expensive and even a cup of seed pods was costly. The famine was so severe that a woman said, "Give me your son so we may eat him today, and tomorrow we will eat my son." When the king heard about this he tore his robes in his distress.

Then the king sent for the Prophet Elisha who came and said, "This is what the LORD says, 'About this time tomorrow a large measure of flour will cost only a small amount and two large measures of barley will also cost the same.'"

The officer on whose arm the king was leaning said, "Look, even if the LORD should open the floodgates of the heavens, could this happen?"

Prophet Elisha answered, "You will see it with your own eyes but you will not eat any of it!"

Now there were four men with leprosy at the entrance of the city gate. They said to each other, "Why stay here until we die? If we say, 'We'll go into the city—the famine is there, and we will die. So let's go over to the camp of the enemy and surrender. If they spare us, we live; if they kill us, then we will die.'"

At dusk the four lepers got up and went to the camp of the enemy. When they reached the edge of the camp, not a man was there, for the LORD had caused the enemy to hear the sound of chariots and horses and a great army. So the enemy army got up and fled in the dusk and abandoned their tents, their horses and donkeys. They left the camp as it was and ran for their lives.

The four lepers reached the edge of the camp and entered into one of the tents. They found food and ate and drank, and carried away silver, gold, and clothes, and went off and hid them. They returned and entered another tent and took some things from it and hid them also.

The four lepers said to each other, "We're not doing right. This is a day of good news and we are keeping it to ourselves. If we wait until daylight, punishment will overtake us. Let's go at once and report this to the king."

So they went and called to the city gatekeepers and told them, "We went to the enemy camp and not a man was there, not even the sound of anyone. Their horses and tents were left just as they were." The gatekeepers shouted the good news, and it was reported to the king.

The king sent two chariots with drivers to find out what happened. The drivers found the road filled with clothing and the enemy's equipment. So the people of the city went out to the camp and plundered it. There was so much food that a large measure of flour and two large measures of barley sold for a small amount just as the prophet had said.

The king put the officer on whose arm he leaned in charge of the city gate. But the people trampled him in the gateway, and he died, just as Prophet Elisha said would happen. The officer had said to Prophet Elisha, "Look, even if the LORD should open the floodgates of the heavens, could this happen?" And Prophet Elisha had replied, "You will see it with your eyes, but you will not eat any of it." And that is exactly what happened, for the people trampled him in the gateway, and he died.

Food for Thought:
1. Can listeners imagine how bad the famine was? Even a donkey's head for food was very costly. A small measure of seed pods was more than a day's wage.
2. What had the women said they would do in order to have food to eat? Have the listeners heard of such a thing?
3. What good news did Prophet Elisha bring to the king?
4. Did the king's officer believe Prophet Elisha or mock him in doubt?
5. What did Prophet Elisha reply to the officer?
6. What decision did the four lepers make? Was their choice a wise one?
7. What did the lepers find when they arrived at the enemy camp?
8. What did the lepers begin to do when they found food?
9. Then what did the lepers decide to do? Did they want to share the good news or keep all the food to themsleves?
10. When the people heard about the food in the enemy tents, what happened?
11. When the king put the officer in charge of the city gate what happened to him?
12. Did the words of Prophet Elisha come true?
13. When God sends good news, should we doubt it like the officer, or believe it and rejoice and thank God for his mercy?
14. Did the four lepers make a good decision? Who were they thinking about—themselves or all the people in the city?

Food for the Heart: "Blessed is the man who trusts in the LORD, whose confidence is in him" (Jer. 17:7).

20. Hezekiah—the Great Passover Celebration

Scripture Base: 2 Kings 18:1-7; 2 Chronicles 29:1-24; 30:1-27

Prepare the Food:

1. Do the listeners have a time when there is special celebration and worship when they also eat together?
2. Do the listeners recall the story of the Passover meal that God commanded in the days of Moses? It was to be celebrated every year as a memorial of the people's release from slavery in Egypt. (If not, retell that story.)

Serve the Meal:

The Great Passover Celebration

Hezekiah was only twenty-five years old when he became king. In the first month he reopened the doors of God's temple that had been closed by his sinful father. King Hezekiah instructed the priests to make themselves ritually clean and then to remove everything that was unclean from the temple. Then the priests reported to King Hezekiah, "We have purified the entire temple of the LORD and returned all the items of worship."

Early the next morning the king gathered the city officials together and went to the temple. There the priests offered many blood sacrifices for the sins of all the people.

King Hezekiah also had all the altars to false gods, idols and worship places destroyed. He purified the city of all things that displeased God. There was no one like him among all the kings, either before him or after him.

Before the reign of King Hezekiah, the people had stopped celebrating the Passover regularly as commanded by God in the days of Moses. So King Hezekiah sent word to all the people of the land to come to Jerusalem to the temple of God to worship and celebrate the Passover festival.

A very large crowd gathered in Jerusalem to celebrate the Feast of Unleavened Bread and the Passover meal that was part of it. They slaughtered the Passover lamb on the appointed day. Some of the people had not properly consecrated themselves but they ate the Passover meal anyway. King Hezekiah prayed for them, asking God to pardon the people because they set their hearts on seeking the LORD, the God of their fathers.

The people celebrated the Feast of Unleavened Bread for seven days with great rejoicing while the priests sang songs praising the LORD. The whole assembly then agreed to celebrate the festival seven more days. So they continued to celebrate joyfully.

King Hezekiah provided a great number of bulls, sheep and goats for the food. So the entire assembly of people rejoiced along with the priests. Since the days of Solomon son of King David there had been nothing like this in Jerusalem. The priests stood to bless the people, and God heard them. For their prayer reached heaven, God's holy dwelling place.

These are the things that King Hezekiah did throughout the land, doing what was good and right and faithful before the LORD his God.

Food for Thought:

1. What was the first thing that young King Hezekiah asked the priests to do?
2. What festival had not been celebrated regularly by the people?
3. After the people gathered in Jerusalem, how long did they celebrate the Feast of Unleavened Bread and the Passover?
4. What did they decide to do after that first week? As they ate the food what did the people do? Were they joyful?

Food for the Heart: "So whether you eat or drink or whatever you do, do it all for the glory of God" (1 Cor. 10:31).

21. Daniel and Friends Eat Wisely

Scripture Base: Daniel 1:1-20

Prepare the Food:
1. If listeners had a choice would they prefer to eat whatever food was set before them or to eat wisely?
2. What advantages might one have by eating wisely?

Serve the Meal:

Daniel and His Friends Eat Wisely

A time came when an enemy of Abraham's descendants carried off members of the royal family to live in another country. The king ordered his chief court officer to bring in some of the young men from among the royal family and nobility. These were young men without any physical defect, who were handsome, showing aptitude for every kind of learning, well informed, quick to understand, and qualified to serve in the king's palace.

The court officer was to teach the young men the language and literature of the new land. The king assigned the young men a daily amount of food and wine from the king's table. They were to be trained for three years and after that to enter the king's service.

Among the young men were four whose names were Daniel, Hananiah, Mishael, and Azariah. They were each given new names by the chief officer.

But Daniel resolved not to defile himself with the royal food and wine. He asked the king's chief officer for permission not to defile himself in this way.

God caused the chief officer to show favor and sympathy to Daniel. But the chief officer told Daniel, "I am afraid of my king, who has assigned your food and drink. Why should he see you looking worse than the other young men your age? The king would then have my head because of you?"

Daniel then said to the guard the chief officer had appointed over Daniel, Hananiah, Mishael, and Azariah, "Please test your servants for ten days: Give us nothing but vegetables to eat and water to drink. Then compare our appearance with that of the young men who eat the royal food. Then treat your servants in accordance with what you see." So the guard agreed to this and tested Daniel and his companions for ten days.

At the end of ten days they looked healthier and better nourished than any of the other young men who ate the royal food. So the guard took away the choice royal food and wine they were to drink and gave them vegetables instead.

To these young men God gave knowledge and understanding of all kinds of literature and learning. Also Daniel could understand visions and dreams of all kinds.

At the end of the time set by the king to bring the young men in, the chief officer presented them before the king. The king talked with Daniel and his companions. In every matter of wisdom and understanding the king found them ten times better than all the magicians and enchanters in his whole kingdom.

Food for Thought:

1. Why did Daniel want to eat only vegetables and drink water instead of the king's food?
2. Why was the guard fearful of letting Daniel and his companions eat only vegetables and drink water?
3. At the end of ten days, who looked healthier, Daniel and his companions, or the other young men?
4. After the time of preparation when Daniel and his companions were brought before the king, what did the king discover?

Food for the Heart: "Why spend money on what is not bread, and your labor on what does not satisfy? Listen, listen to me, and eat what is good, and your soul will delight in the richest of fare" (Isa. 55:2).

22. Jeremiah— A Starving Prophet

Scripture Base: Jeremiah 1:4, 7-8; 7:1-3; 19:14-15; 20:1-2; 26:7-8; 37:2-31

Prepare the Food:

1. Tell about how God called prophets to be his spokesman to the people, to call the people to repent of their sins and return to Him as their God.
2. Talk about the suffering that prophets often faced because the people did not like to hear their words.

Serve the Meal:

Jeremiah—A Starving Prophet

The word of the LORD came to the Prophet Jeremiah saying, "Before I formed you in the womb I knew you, before you were born I set you apart; I appointed you to be a prophet to the nations. You must go to everyone I send you and say whatever I command you. Do not be afraid of them, for I am with you and will rescue you."

This is the word of the LORD that came to Prophet Jeremiah: "Stand at the gate of the LORD'S house and proclaim this message: "Hear the word of the LORD, all you people who come through these gates to worship the LORD. This is what the LORD Almighty says, 'Reform your ways and your actions, and I will let you live in this place.'"

Again Prophet Jeremiah said to all the people, "This is what the LORD says, 'Listen! I am going to bring on this city and the villages around it every disaster I pronounced against them, because they were stiff-necked and would not listen to my words.'"

When the chief officer in the temple heard Prophet Jeremiah prophesying these things, he had Jeremiah beaten and put in stocks. Later the priests, the prophets and the people heard Jeremiah speak. But as soon as he finished telling all the people everything the LORD had commanded him to say, the priests, the prophets and the people seized him and said, "You must die!"

Neither the king, his attendants, nor any of the people paid any attention to the words of the LORD spoken by Prophet Jeremiah. At that time Prophet Jeremiah was free to come and go among the people. But when Prophet Jeremiah started to leave the city, he was arrested and accused of deserting to the enemy. Jeremiah protested, but the people beat him and put him in a cell at the secretary's house that had been made into a prison where Jeremiah remained a long time.

Finally the king sent for Prophet Jeremiah and asked if there were any word from the LORD? Then Jeremiah said to the king, "What crime have I committed against you or this people, that you put me in prison? Do not send me back to that house where I was kept, or I will die there."

So the king gave orders for Prophet Jeremiah to be placed in the courtyard of the guard and given bread from the street of bakers each day until all the bread in the city was gone. Later Prophet Jeremiah was seized again and put into a deep cistern where he sank into the mud. Some friends came to rescue him because they were afraid he would starve when there is no longer any bread in the city. They pulled the prophet to safety before he died. Prophet Jeremiah remained in the courtyard of the guard until the city was captured.

Food for Thought:
1. What did God want Prophet Jeremiah to do?
2. Did Prophet Jeremiah obey God to tell the people what God said?
3. What happened as a result of the prophet's words?
4. What punishments did the Prophet Jeremiah suffer?
5. Did God rescue him each time?
6. What food was he given to eat as long as it was available?

Food for the Heart: "I will rescue you on that day... because you trust in me, declares the LORD" (Jer. 39:17b, 18b).

23. When Jesus Fasted in the Desert

Scripture Base: Matthew 4:1-11; Mark 1:12-13; Luke 4:1-13

Prepare the Food:

1. Do listeners have a custom of fasting for some ceremonial purpose or spiritual purpose?
2. What do they consider to be the purpose of fasting?
3. When fasting, does this increase the hunger for food?

Serve the Meal:

When Jesus Fasted in the Desert

Then Jesus, filled with God's Holy Spirit, returned from the river where he was baptized. Immediately, the Holy Spirit led Jesus into the desert with the wild beasts, where he remained forty days to be tempted by Satan, the devil.

Jesus ate nothing during the whole time. After fasting at length for forty days and nights, Jesus was very hungry. So the tempter, Satan, said to Jesus, "Since you are the Son of God, command these stones to become bread."

Jesus replied to Satan, "It is written, 'Man shall not live on bread alone, but on every word that comes from the mouth of God'" (Deut. 8:3).

Then Satan took Jesus into the holy city, Jerusalem, and set him on top of the temple. Satan said, "Since you are the Son of God, throw yourself down from here. For it is written, 'He will command his angels to guard you and carry you in their hands, so you won't injure your foot on a stone'" (Ps. 91:11-12).

Jesus replied, "It is written, 'You are not to put the Lord your God to the test'" (Deut. 6:16).

Then Satan led Jesus up a high mountain. In a single moment Satan showed Jesus all the kingdoms of the world in all their glory. And Satan said to Jesus, "All this power and splendor I'll give you. It has been turned over to me and I can give it to anyone I want. So bow down and worship me, and it will be yours."

Jesus replied to Satan," Be gone, Satan! For it is written, 'Worship the Lord your God and serve him only'" (Deut. 6:13).

So Satan, after trying every kind of temptation, left Jesus until another opportune time. Angels came and ministered to Jesus.

Food for Thought:

1. Why do listeners think God wanted to cause Jesus to suffer and be tempted?
2. Did Jesus use his authority over nature to turn the stones into bread like Satan asked?
3. In the Holy Scriptures there was a promise to protect the Messiah (Jesus) from harm. What did Jesus have to say about putting God to a foolish test? (Psa. 91:11-12).
4. Why did Jesus refuse to bow down and worship Satan? Who really owns the kingdoms of the world? Who made the world and all the people in the kingdoms? Did Jesus give a wise answer?
5. Jesus ate the food that people gave him. But he did not use his authority and power from God to make food.
6. If Jesus came to your house today, would listeners invite him to come and eat with them and their family?
7. How did Jesus' fasting affect each of us? (he suffered like we suffer)

Food for the Heart: "Because he himself suffered when he was tempted, he is able to help those being tempted" (Heb. 2:18).

24. Eating with Unwashed Hands

Scripture Base: Matthew 15:1-20; Mark 7:1-23; John 7:1

Prepare the Food:
1. Do listeners wash their hands before eating? How do they do wash?
2. In many places people have a clean hand and a "dirty" hand. Is it okay to eat with the clean hand? How about the "dirty" hand?

Serve the Meal:

Eating With Unwashed Hands

Jesus was continuing his ministry as he traveled about the country. One day some Pharisees and teachers of the law surrounded him. When they saw Jesus' disciples eating with unwashed hands, they began criticizing the disciples. For the Pharisees and the rest of the religiously careful people don't eat until they ceremonially wash their hands. This was a tradition handed down from their ancestors. When they came from the marketplace, they didn't eat until they ceremonially washed themselves. They also observed other ancient customs such as washing of cups and pots and bronze utensils.

So the Pharisees and teachers of the law asked Jesus, "Why do your disciples disregard the tradition of our ancestors? See, they do not wash their hands before eating."

"You hypocrites!" Jesus answered. "The prophet spoke about you when he wrote,

> This people honor me with their lips, but their heart is far from me. They worship me in vain and teach human regulations as if they were divine commands.
>
> You disregard the commands of God and instead obey human traditions, such as the washing of pots and cups."

When Jesus had called everyone together, he said, "Listen to me and understand, all of you. What goes into a person's mouth can never make him unclean. What makes him unclean are the words that come out of his mouth."

One of the disciples asked Jesus to explain the meaning. "Are you so dull?" Jesus asked. "Don't you see that whatever enters the mouth goes into the stomach and out of the body? But the things that come out of the mouth come from the heart, and these make a man unclean. For out of the heart come evil thoughts, murder, adultery, sexual immorality, theft, false testimony and slander. These are what make a man unclean; but eating with unwashed hands does not make him unclean."

Food for Thought:

1. What is worse, unclean hands or an unclean heart?
2. Why is it so important to have a clean pure heart?
3. What kinds of things come from an impure heart?
4. Are the listeners' hearts clean? Do they know someone with an unclean heart? What can be done about it?
5. Read for the listeners Genesis 6:5-6.
6. What does God think about unclean hearts?
7. How can one's heart be made clean? Who could do it?

Food for the Heart: "Create in me a pure heart, O God, and renew a steadfast spirit within me" (Psa. 51:10).

25. Eating with Sinners At Matthew's House

Scripture Base: Matthew 9:9-17; Mark 2:13-22; Luke 5:27-39

Prepare the Food:

1. Among the listeners who are the "bad" people or people they would call "sinners?"
2. Is it possible to have fellowship or eat with these "sinners?"
3. What if other people considered the listeners "sinners"? Would the listeners be honored if someone important ate with them?

Serve the Meal:

Eating With Sinners At Matthew's House

One day Jesus saw a tax collector named Matthew sitting at the tax collector's booth. Jesus said to Matthew, "Follow me." Matthew got up, left everything, and followed Jesus.

Then Matthew held a great meal for Jesus at his house. Jesus was joined by his disciples, and a large number of tax collectors, and other people of low reputation, for there were many people following Jesus. When the Pharisees and teachers of the law saw Jesus eating with these tax collectors and other outcasts, they began speaking critically to Jesus' disciples. "Why do you eat and drink with tax collectors and sinners? And why does your teacher?"

When Jesus heard what the Pharisees and teachers of the law were saying, He replied, "It is not the healthy who need a doctor, but the sick. I have not come to call the righteous, but sinners to repentance" (Luke 5:31).

At that time the disciples of the Prophet John, as well as the Pharisees, were fasting. John's disciples approached Jesus and asked, "Why do we and the disciples of the Pharisees frequently fast, but your disciples do not fast?"

Jesus answered, "How can the guests of the bridegroom fast while he is with them? They cannot, so long as they have the bridegroom with them. But the time will come when the bridegroom will be taken from them, and on that day they will fast."

Food for Thought:
1. Who called Matthew's friends "sinners?"
2. What makes a person a "sinner?" How can one know if they are a "sinner?"
3. Why did Jesus want to eat with these people? Did Jesus call them "healthy" or "sick?"
4. How could Jesus make the sick people get well?
5. Why did Jesus say that his disciples were not fasting like the disciples of the Pharisees and the disciples of the Prophet John?
6. Who is the bridegroom Jesus mentioned?
7. What did Jesus mean when he said, "...the bridegroom will be taken from them?"
8. Do listeners think that Jesus would come to eat with them? Would Jesus think they were worthy for fellowship like that?

Food for the Heart: "For the Son of Man came to seek and to save what was lost" (Luke 19:10).

26. Hungering for Righteousness

Scripture Base: Matthew 4:23-25; 5:1-11; 6:16-18, 25-27; 7:15-20, 28-29, 31-33

Prepare the Food:
1. What do listeners hunger for? Is it food? A better life?
2. Do listeners know what *righteousness* is?

Serve the Meal:

Hungering for Righteousness

Jesus had gone throughout the countryside teaching in the places of worship, preaching good news about the kingdom of heaven, and healing every disease and sickness among the people. News about Jesus spread everywhere and people brought to Jesus all who were ill with various diseases, those suffering severe pain, the demon-possessed, and those paralyzed. And Jesus healed them all. Large crowds followed Jesus. When Jesus saw the crowds, he went up on a mountainside and sat down. His disciples came to Jesus and he taught them:

> Blessed are the poor in spirit for theirs is the kingdom of heaven.
>
> Blessed are those who mourn, for they will be comforted.
>
> Blessed are the meek, for they will inherit the earth.
>
> *Blessed are those who hunger and thirst for righteousness, for they will be filled.*
>
> Blessed are the merciful, for they will be shown mercy.
>
> Blessed are the pure in heart, for they will see God.
>
> Blessed are the peacemakers, for they will be called the sons of God.
>
> Blessed are those who are persecuted because of righteousness, for theirs is the kingdom of heaven.
>
> Blessed are you when people insult you, persecute you and falsely say all kinds of evil against you be-

cause of me. Rejoice and be glad, because great is your reward in heaven.

When you fast, do not look somber as the hypocrites do, for they disfigure their faces to show men they are fasting. I tell you the truth, they have received their reward in full. But when you fast, anoint your head and wash your face, so it will not be obvious to men that you are fasting, but only to your Father in heaven who sees what is done in secret and will reward you.

Therefore I tell you, do not worry about your life, what you will eat or drink; or about your body, or what you will wear. Is not life more important than food, and the body more important than clothes? Look at the birds of the air; they do not sow or reap or store away in barns, and yet your heavenly Father feeds them. Are you not much more valuable than they? Who of you by worrying can add a single hour to his life?

So do not worry, saying, 'What shall we eat?' or 'What shall we drink?' or 'What shall we wear?' For the unbelievers run after these things, and your heavenly Father knows you need them. But seek first the kingdom of God and his righteousness, and all these things will be given to you.

Food for Thought:
1. What could it mean for one to hunger and thirst for righteousness?
2. Who could satisfy that hunger for righteousness?
3. Who could make us righteous?

Food for the Heart: "For just as through the disobedience of the one man the many were made sinners, so also through the obedience of the one man the many will be made righteous" (Rom. 5:19).

27. The Sinful Woman At Simon's Supper

Scripture Base: Luke 7:36-50

Prepare the Food:

1. If listeners could be forgiven for all their sins or trespasses, what would they be willing to do in return?
2. Who can forgive sin?
3. Does anyone need to have his or her sin forgiven?

Serve the Meal:

The Sinful Woman at Simon's Supper

Then one of the Pharisees named Simon asked Jesus to come to his house for a meal. So Jesus went to the house and was reclining at the table according to their custom. Then a woman from the city who had lived a sinful life learned that Jesus was eating at the Pharisee's house. She came bringing a jar of perfume. The woman stood behind Jesus weeping and her tears fell on Jesus' feet. The woman began to wash Jesus' feet with her tears and wipe them with her hair. She began kissing the feet of Jesus and anointing Jesus' feet with her perfume.

When Simon, the Pharisee, who had invited Jesus saw this, he said to himself, "If this man were a prophet, he would know who is touching him and what kind of a woman she is. She is a sinner!"

Jesus answered, "Simon, I have something to tell you."

"Tell me, teacher," Simon replied.

Then Jesus told this story: "Two men owed money to a moneylender. One owed him a very large amount of money. The other man owed only a small amount of money. Neither man had the money to repay the moneylender. So the moneylender canceled the debts of both men. Now which of the men loved the moneylender more?"

Simon replied, "I suppose the one who had the larger debt forgiven."

"You have judged correctly," Jesus said.

Then Jesus turned toward the woman and said to Simon, "Do you see this woman? I came into your house. You did not give me any water to wash my feet. But this woman has wet my feet with her tears and wiped them with her hair. Simon, you did not give me a kiss of greeting, but this woman has not stopped kissing my feet. You did not put any fragrant oil on my head, but she has poured perfume on my feet. Therefore I tell you, her many sins have been forgiven—for she loved much. But he who has been forgiven little loves little."

Then Jesus said to the woman, "Your sins are forgiven."

The other guests began to say among themselves, "Who is this who even forgives sins?"

Jesus said to the woman, "Your faith has saved you; go in peace."

Food for Thought:

1. Talk about why Simon might have invited Jesus to his house? (perhaps to test him or see what Jesus was like)
2. Why did the woman come to Simon's house? Did she know Jesus was there?
3. What did she do at Jesus' feet? What might be symbolized by touching Jesus' feet with her hair? (bowing in humility and worship)
4. Did Simon think this was a good thing to do?
5. In the story Jesus told, who loved the moneylender more?
6. Who loved Jesus more—Simon or the sinful woman?
7. Did Jesus forgive her sins? What blessing did Jesus give the woman? (Go in peace.)

Food for the Heart: "If we confess our sins, he is faithful and just and will forgive us our sins and purify us from all unrighteousness" (1 John 1:9).

28. Lazarus—A Starving Beggar

Scripture Base: Luke 16:14-15, 19-31

Prepare the Food:

1. Does anyone know what it is like to beg for food?
2. What happens when we die? Where do we go? Does it make any difference what we believed or did in this life?

Serve the Meal:

Lazarus—A Starving Beggar

The Pharisees, who loved money, heard all that Jesus said and were mocking him. Jesus said to them, "You are the ones who justify yourselves in the eyes of men, but God knows your hearts. What is highly valued among men is detestable in God's sight."

Then Jesus began to tell this story: "There was a rich man who was dressed in expensive clothing and lived in great luxury every day. At his gate was laid a beggar named Lazarus who was covered with sores. Lazarus longed to eat the food scraps that fell from the rich man's table. Even the dogs came and licked poor Lazarus' sores.

The time came when Lazarus died and angels carried him to Abraham's side. The rich man also died and was buried. In hell, where he was in great torment, the rich man looked up and saw Abraham far away with the beggar Lazarus by his side. So the rich man called to him, "Father Abraham, have pity on me and send Lazarus to dip the tip of his finger in water and cool my tongue. I am suffering in this place.'"

But Abraham replied, "Son, remember that in your lifetime you received your good things, while Lazarus received bad things. But now Lazarus is comforted here and you are in agony. And besides all this, between us and you a great chasm has been fixed, so those who want to go from here to you cannot; no one can cross over from there to us."

The rich man answered, "Father Abraham, then I beg you to send Lazarus to my father's house, for I have five brothers.

Let Lazarus warn them, so they will not also come to this place of torment."

Abraham replied, "Your brothers have Moses and the Prophets: let your brothers listen to them."

Then the rich man said, "No, father Abraham, but if someone from the dead goes to warn them, they will repent."

Abraham said, "If your brothers do not listen to Moses and the Prophets, they will not be convinced even if someone rises from the dead."

Food for Thought:

1. Why did Jesus tell this story about these two men?
2. Which man had all his needs in this life? Which did not?
3. When the men died where did each go? What do listeners suppose was the difference?
4. What did the rich man want Abraham to have Lazarus do for him?
5. Could Abraham help the rich man?
6. Then what did the rich man want Abraham to do?
7. Who did the rich man's brothers have to warn them?
8. Would the brothers listen?
9. What might be the difference between poor Lazarus and the rich man while still living? Could it be that Lazarus paid attention to the words of the Prophets even though he was poor and sick?
10. Do listeners believe that Lazarus is no longer starving?
11. Consider that there were actually two rich men in this story. Abraham was also very wealthy, yet he was not suffering. Read Heb. 11:11-13.

Food for the Heart: "But these are written that you may believe that Jesus is the Christ, the Son of God, and that by believing you may have life in his name" (John 20:31).

29. The Rich Fool

Scripture Base: Luke 12:13, 15-21

Prepare the Food:
1. Do any of the listeners consider themselves to be rich?
2. What makes a man rich? Or poor?
3. What is a danger of being rich? Who is the most important person to someone who is rich?
4. What might make a rich man behave like a fool?

Serve the Meal:

The Rich Fool

Someone in the crowd said to Jesus, "Teacher, tell my brother to divide the inheritance with me."

Jesus replied, "Watch out! Be on your guard against all kinds of greed: a man's life does not consist in the abundance of his possessions."

Then Jesus told the people this parable:

> The land of a certain rich man produced a very good crop. The man thought to himself, "What shall I do? I have no place to store all my harvest."
>
> Then the rich man said, "This is what I'll do. I will tear down my barns and build bigger ones, and there I will store all my grain and my goods. And I'll say to myself, 'You have plenty of good things laid up for many years. Take life easy; eat, drink, and be merry.'"
>
> But God said to the rich man, "You fool! This very night your life will be demanded from you. Then who will get what you have prepared for yourself?"

Then Jesus said to the people, "This is how it will be with anyone who stores up things for himself, but is not rich toward God."

Food for Thought:

1. At the beginning of the story what did the man ask Jesus?
2. What did Jesus warn the man?
3. Who gave the rich man his good harvest? Who makes the crops to grow by sending rain and sunshine?
4. Who was the rich man thinking about when he had a very good harvest?
5. Who should the rich man be thinking about if he had so much food? What should the rich man do with his extra food?
6. What does God think about greed and selfishness?
7. If God made everything and already owns everything, how can one be rich toward God?
8. Are listeners rich toward God? Are they rich toward others who live in their villages or cities?

Food for the Heart: "Command those who are rich in this present world not to be arrogant nor to put their hope in wealth, which is so uncertain, but to put their hope in God, who richly provides us with everything for our enjoyment (1 Tim. 6:17).

30. A Starving Son Who Repented

Scripture Base: Luke 15:1-2, 11-32

Prepare the Food:
1. Have any of the listeners ever dishonored their fathers in some way?
2. What is the local practice about dividing up the family inheritance? Does anyone get a larger share?
3. What if someone asked for their share while their father was still living?

Serve the Meal:

A Starving Son Who Repented

The tax collectors and sinners were all gathering around to hear Jesus. But the Pharisees and the teachers of the law muttered, "This man welcomes sinners and eats with them."
So Jesus told them this story:

> There was a man who had two sons. The younger son said to his father, "Father, give me my share of the inheritance." So the father divided his property between his two sons.
>
> Not long after that, the younger son got together all he had received from his father and set off for a distant country. There the younger son squandered his wealth in wild living. After he had spent all he had, there was a severe famine in that whole country. The younger son began to be in great need.
>
> So the younger son went and hired himself out to a citizen of that country, who sent him to the fields to feed his pigs. The younger son longed to fill his stomach with the pods that the pigs were eating, but no one gave him anything to eat.
>
> When the younger son came to his senses, he said, "How many of my father's hired men have food to spare, and here I am starving to death! I will set out and go back to my father and say to him: 'Father, I have sinned against heaven and against you. I am no longer worthy to be called your son; make me

like one of your hired men.'" So the son got up and went to his father.

But while the younger son was still a long way off, his father saw him and was filled with compassion for him. The father ran to his son, threw his arms around his son and kissed him.

The son said to his father, "Father, I have sinned against heaven and against you. I am no longer worthy to be called your son."

But the father said to his servants, "Quick! Bring the best robe and put it on him. Put a ring on his finger and sandals on his feet. Bring meat and prepare it. Let's have a feast and celebrate. For this son of mine was dead and is alive again; he was lost and is now found." So they began to celebrate.

Meanwhile, the older son was in the field. When he came near the house, he heard music and dancing. So he called one of the servants and asked him what was going on. The servant replied, "Your brother has come, and your father has prepared a feast because he has your brother back safe."

The older brother became angry and refused to go in. So his father went out and pleaded with him. But the older son answered his father, "Look! All these years I've been slaving for you and never disobeyed your orders. Yet you never gave me even a young goat so I could celebrate with my friends. But when this son of yours who has squandered all your property with prostitutes comes home, you prepare a feast for him!"

The father replied, "My son, you are always with me. And everything I have is yours. But we had to celebrate and be glad, because this brother of yours was dead and is alive again, he was lost and is found."

Jesus told the people listening to him, "In the same way, I tell you, there is rejoicing in the presence of the angels of God over one sinner who repents."

Food for Thought:
1. What was more valuable to the younger son: the relationship with his father or the inheritance he wanted?
2. What did the younger son begin to do with his part of the inheritance?
3. What soon happened to the younger son's money?
4. Who was willing to help the younger son when his money was gone and a famine came in the land?
5. What work did the younger son find to do? (mention that among the younger son's family that pigs were considered unclean animals and this was very shameful work)
6. What did the younger son decide to do? What would he ask his father?
7. When the father saw his younger son coming, what did he do?
8. Did the younger son try to confess his sin before his father?
9. What did the father tell the servants to do?
10. Why was there rejoicing at the home of the younger son?
11. What was the older son's complaint?
12. What did the father tell the older son about the younger son?
13. What did Jesus say about those who repent?

Food for the Heart: "Godly sorrow brings repentance that leads to salvation and leaves no regret, but worldly sorrow brings death" (2 Cor.7:10).

31. Food for the Hungry Multitude

Scripture Base: Matthew 14:13-21; Mark 6:30-44; Luke 9:10-17; John 6:1-15

Prepare the Food:
1. Do listeners know someone who is concerned about their hunger?
2. Would that person be able to feed the listeners and their families? How would they do it?

Serve the Meal:

Food for the Hungry Multitude

Jesus said to his disciples, "Come away with me to a wilderness place and rest for a little while." Jesus took his disciples by boat to the other side of the lake. But the crowds of people saw Jesus leaving, many recognized him, so the crowds hurried on foot in that direction. They followed Jesus because they saw the miraculous signs when Jesus healed the sick. The people arrived before Jesus and were waiting for him. When Jesus saw the great crowd, he was moved with compassion because the people were like sheep having no shepherd. So Jesus welcomed them and began to teach the people many things. Jesus talked with them about the Kingdom of God and healed those who needed healing.

Now it was late in the day. Jesus went up on the mountain and sat down with his disciples. The disciples said to Jesus, "This is a remote place, and it's already very late. Send the people away so they can go to the villages and buy something to eat."

Jesus answered the disciples, "You give them something to eat."

"But that would take eight months of a man's wages! Are we to go and spend that much on bread and give it to them to eat?" the disciples asked.

"How many loaves do you have?" Jesus asked. "Go and see."

When the disciples found out, they said, "Five loaves and two fish."

"Bring the food to me," Jesus said and then asked the disciples to have all the people sit down in groups on the green grass. The people sat in groups of fifty and one hundred.

Jesus took the five loaves and two fish and looked up to heaven. He gave thanks and then broke the loaves and gave the pieces to the disciples to give the people. Jesus also took the two fish and blessed and divided the fish for the disciples to give the people.

The crowd ate and were satisfied. Afterward Jesus said to his disciples to gather up what is left so that nothing is lost. The disciples picked up twelve basketfuls of broken pieces of bread and fish left by those who had eaten. The people Jesus fed were about five thousand men, besides the women and children.

Food for Thought:
1. When Jesus saw the large crowd of people following him, what did he feel toward the people?
2. After teaching the people and healing all who needed healing, what did Jesus tell his disciples to do?
3. Did the disciples think it was possible to feed so many people?
4. How much food did the disciples find among the people?
5. Did Jesus think that was enough? What did Jesus say?
6. What did Jesus do with the loaves and fish?
7. Was the food enough for the people to eat?
8. What does this tell us about Jesus? What other ways could Jesus feed us?

Food for the Heart: "I am the living bread that came down from heaven, if a man eats of this bread he will live forever" (John 6:31a)

32. Jesus—the Bread Come Down from Heaven

Scripture Base: John 6:25-51

Prepare the Food:

1. Do listeners know of a food to eat so that one would never be hungry again?
2. If listeners heard about such a food, would they want to have it? Here is a story about living bread that satisfies.

Serve the Meal:

Jesus—the Bread Come Down from Heaven

After Jesus fed the great multitude of people along with his disciples, they got into a boat and again crossed the lake. When the crowds came searching for him and found Jesus, they said, "Rabbi (Teacher), when did you get here?"

Jesus answered, "I tell you the truth, you are looking for me, not because you saw miraculous signs, but because you ate the loaves of bread and had your fill. Do not work for food that spoils, but for the food that endures to eternal life, which the Son of Man will give you."

The people asked Jesus, "What miraculous sign will you give that we may see it and believe you? Our forefathers ate the manna in the desert; as it is written: He gave them bread from heaven to eat."

Jesus said to the people, "I tell you the truth, it is not Moses who has given you bread from heaven, but it is my Father who gives you the true bread from heaven. For the bread of God is he who comes down from heaven and gives life to the world."

The people said, "Sir, from now on give us this bread."

Then Jesus declared, "I am the bread of life. He who comes to me will never go hungry, and he who believes in me will never be thirsty. But as I told you, you have seen me and still you do not believe. I have come down from heaven not to do my will, but to do the will of him who sent me. For my

Father's will is that everyone who looks to the Son and believes in him shall have eternal life, and I will raise him up on the last day."

At this the people began to grumble about Jesus because he said,

> I am the bread that came down from heaven. I am the bread of life. Our forefathers ate the manna in the desert, yet they died. But here is the bread that comes down from heaven, which a man may eat and not die. I am the living bread that came down from haven. If a man eats of this bread, he will live forever. Just as the living Father sent me and I live because of the Father, so the one who feeds on me will live because of me. This is the bread that came down from heaven.

Food for Thought:

1. Why were the people following Jesus? (to get bread)
2. Where does true bread come from? Who gives it?
3. Who did Jesus say he was? What do you think Jesus meant by this?
4. Jesus said that if one eats his bread that the person will live _____?
5. Should we be looking for this living bread? Where can we find it?
6. Do listeners believe the words of Jesus in this story?
7. Would they like some of this living bread?

Food for the Heart: "While they were eating, Jesus took bread, gave thanks and broke it, and gave it to his disciples, saying, 'Take it; this is my body'" (Mark 14:22).

33. The Great Feast And Refused Invitations

Scripture Base: Luke 14:15-24

Prepare the Food:

1. If listeners were invited to a wonderful feast, would they go, or would they make excuses not to go?
2. If listeners prepared a feast and invited their neighbors but no one came, what would they do?

Serve the Meal:

The Great Feast And Refused Invitations

One worship day Jesus had gone to eat in the house of a prominent Pharisee. One of the guests at the table said to Jesus, "Blessed is the man who will eat at the feast of the kingdom of God."

Jesus replied:

> A certain man was preparing a great feast and invited many guests. At the time of the feast the man sent his servant to tell those who had been invited, "Come, for the food is now ready."
>
> But the invited guests began to make excuses. The first said, "I have just bought a field, and I must go and see it. Please excuse me."
>
> Another invited guest said, "I have just bought five yoke of oxen, and I'm on my way to try them out. Please excuse me."
>
> Still another invited guest said, "I just got married, so I can't come."
>
> The servant returned and reported this to his master. Then the owner of the house became angry and ordered his servant, "Go out quickly into the streets and alleys of the town and bring in the poor, the crippled, the blind and the lame."

Later the servant said, "Sir, what you ordered has been done, but there is still room for more."

Then the master told his servant, "Go out to the roads and country lanes and compel the people to come in, so that my house will be full. I tell you, not one of those men who were invited will get a taste of my feast."

Food for Thought:

1. Remember the words of the man who spoke to Jesus. Why do listeners think Jesus told this story? Could it be that a feast is being prepared and invitations have gone out, but many will refuse the invitation?
2. What were some of the excuses the people gave for not coming? Were these good excuses, or do listeners think perhaps the people did not want to go to the feast?
3. When the man heard the excuses from the people, what did he command his servant to do?
4. When there was still more room at the feast, what did the man tell his servant to do?
5. What did the man say about his house? I want my house to be _____?
6. What about those who were invited but did not go? Will they get any of the feast?
7. If listeners were invited to such a wonderful feast, would they go or make excuses not to go?
8. God's Word says: On this mountain the Lord Almighty will prepare a feast of rich food for all peoples, a banquet of the best meat and drink (Isa. 25:6).
9. The promise says that it is "for all peoples." Does that include each of the listeners?

Food for the Heart: "So Christ was sacrificed once to take away the sins of many people; and he will appear a second time, not to bear sin, but to bring salvation to those who are waiting for him" (Heb.9:28).

34. The Last Supper—Fellowship, Covenant & Betrayal

Scripture Base: Psalm 41:9; Matthew 26:28; Mark 10:33; 14:12-26; John 13:33, 36; 14:1-4, 6, 10, 23; 27

Prepare the Food:

1. What does it mean to listeners to eat along with their families and friends? Fellowship? Joy? Sharing?
2. Jesus wanted to eat a last meal with his disciples. It was a special time—the Feast of Unleavened Bread—when the Passover Meal was eaten. Jesus was going to tell his disciples what he was going to do very soon.
3. Listen carefully to see what this story means for the listeners.

Serve the Meal:

The Last Supper—Fellowship
Covenant & Betrayal

During the days of King David, he made a prophecy that said: "Even my close friend, whom I trusted, he who shares my bread, has lifted up his heel against me" (Ps. 41:9).

Many times Jesus told his disciples what was going to happen to him. As they were on their way to Jerusalem Jesus again took his twelve disciples aside and told them what was going to happen to him. Jesus said: "We are going to Jerusalem, and the Son of man will be betrayed to the chief priests and teachers of the law. They will condemn him to death and will hand him over to the Gentiles, who will mock him and spit on him, flog him and kill him. Three days later he will rise."

On the first day of the Feast of Unleavened Bread, when it was customary to sacrifice the Passover lamb, Jesus' disciples asked him, "Where do you want us to go and make preparations for you to eat the Passover?" The Passover meal was a lamb roasted whole without breaking any of its bones, unleavened bread, a dip of salt water and bitter herbs and drink made from crushed grapes.

So Jesus sent two of his disciples and told them, "Go into the city, and a man carrying a jar of water will meet you. Follow him. Say to the owner of the house he enters, 'The Teacher asks: Where is the guest room, where I may eat the Passover with my disciples?' He will show you a large upper room, furnished and ready. Make preparations for us there." The disciples went into the city and prepared the Passover.

When evening came, Jesus arrived with the twelve disciples. While they were eating, Jesus took bread, gave thanks and broke it, and gave it to his disciples and said, "Take it; this is my body."

Then Jesus took the cup of drink, gave thanks and offered the cup to the disciples and they all drank from it. Jesus said, "This cup is my blood of the new covenant, which is poured out for the forgiveness of the sins of many."

Jesus said to his disciples, "I tell you the truth, one of you will betray me—one who is eating with me." The disciples were sad to hear this and were asking who it was.

Jesus said, "It is one of the Twelve; one who dips bread into the bowl with me." Then Jesus took a piece of bread and dipped it into the bowl and handed it to the disciple named Judas who took the bread. As soon as Judas had taken the bread, he went out to betray Jesus.

Afterward Jesus told his disciples,

> I will be with you only a little longer...Where I am going, you cannot follow now, but you will follow later... Do not let your hearts be troubled. Trust in God; trust also in me. In my Father's house are many rooms...I am going there to prepare a place for you. And if I go and prepare a place for you, I will come back and take you to be with me...I am the way and the truth and the life. No ones comes to the Father except through me...The words I say to you are not just my own words. Rather, it is the Father, living in me, who is doing his work.

Then Jesus said,

> If anyone loves me, he will obey my teaching. My Father will love him, and we will come to him and

make our home with him...Peace I leave with you; my peace I give you. I do not give it to you as the world gives. Do not let your hearts be troubled and do not be afraid.

After Jesus prayed for his disciples and for himself and all believers in the world; they sang a hymn, and then went outs to a quiet garden to pray.

Food for Thought:

1. What did the prophecy say would happen to Jesus? Who would do it?
2. Did Jesus know what was going to happen to him?
3. What did Jesus say to the disciple who was going to betray him?
4. When Jesus blessed the bread and gave it to his disciples, what did he tell them?
5. When Jesus blessed the cup of drink and gave it to his disciples, what did he tell them?
6. What did Jesus say that he was going away to do?
7. What did Jesus promise his disciples that he would do after preparing a place for them?
8. What did Jesus want his disciples to do to show they loved him?
9. What meaning does this story have for the listeners? Talk about what it means.
10. Recall when Jesus said he was the "bread come down from heaven." What do the listeners think Jesus meant when he said, "This is my body. Take and eat."
11. What did Jesus say about the cup of drink? Could it be for the listeners' sins, too?
12. Does this story help listeners to understand who Jesus is?
13. If there is time and interest, tell the listeners the rest of the story of Jesus, his arrest and trial, his crucifixion and death, and his resurrection. If the JESUS Film is avail-

able, this will visually illustrate the story for listeners. If there is interest to hear more of these stories, then make arrangements to tell the stories of Jesus one-by-one and give time for listeners to talk about each story or for you to teach from the stories.

Food for the Heart: "Jesus Christ, the Righteous One. He is the atoning sacrifice for our sins, and not only for ours but also for the sins of the whole world" (1 John 2:2).

35. Jesus—Do You Have Anything to Eat?

Scripture Base: Luke 24:13-49; Mark 16:14

Prepare the Table:

1. After Jesus was crucified he was raised from the grave on the third day just as he said. Many people saw Jesus. There were some women followers who went to put spices on Jesus' body. But Jesus wasn't in the tomb. Jesus appeared to one called Mary Magdalene, then to the disciple Peter, then to two more followers walking along the road, later that night to his disciples gathered in a room and a few days later to more than 500 people.
2. This story takes place in the evening of the day that Jesus was raised from the grave. Jesus had walked and talked with two followers and then appeared in the room with his disciples. What would the listeners have done if they had been present?

Serve the Meal:

Jesus—Do you Have Anything to Eat?

On the day that Jesus was raised from the dead, two of his followers were going to a village called Emmaus seven miles from Jerusalem. The two men were talking about everything that had happened. As they talked and discussed these things between each other, Jesus himself came up and walked along with them. But the two men did not recognize Jesus who asked them, "What are you discussing together as you walk along?"

The two men stopped. Their faces were downcast. One of the men asked Jesus, "Are you the only one living in Jerusalem who doesn't know the things that have happened in these days?"

"What things?" Jesus asked.

They replied, "About Jesus of Nazareth. He was a prophet, powerful in word and deed before God and all the people. The chief priests and our rulers handed him over to be sentenced to death, and they crucified him. We had hoped that he was the one who would redeem our land. It is the third day since this took place. Some of our women amazed us. They went to his tomb early this morning but didn't find his body. They told us they saw a vision of angels who said Jesus was alive. Then some of our companions went to the tomb and found it was just as the women had said, but they did not see Jesus."

Jesus said to the two men, "How foolish you are, and how slow of heart to believe all the prophets have spoken! Did not the Christ have to suffer these things and then enter his glory?" Beginning with Moses and all the Prophets, Jesus explained to the men what was said in all the Scriptures concerning himself.

As they approached the village where the men were going, Jesus acted as if he were going farther. But the two men urged Jesus strongly, "Stay with us, for it is nearly evening." So Jesus went in to stay with the men.

When Jesus was at the table with the men, he took bread, gave thanks, and broke it and began to give it to them. Then the men's eyes were opened, and they recognized Jesus, and he disappeared from their sight. They said to each other, "Our hearts were burning within us while he talked with us on the road and opened the Scriptures to us."

The two men got up and quickly returned to Jerusalem and found the disciples gathered together. The men told what had happened on the road and how they recognized Jesus when he broke the bread when they sat down to eat.

While they were still talking about this, Jesus himself stood among them and said, "Peace be with you."

The disciples were startled and frightened. They thought they were seeing a ghost. Jesus said to them, "Why are you troubled, and why do doubts rise in your minds? Look at my hands and feet. It is I myself! Touch me and see; a ghost does not have flesh and bones, as you see I have."

When Jesus had said this to the disciples, he showed them his hands and feet. And while they still did not believe it because of joy and amazement, Jesus asked them, "Do you have anything to eat? The disciples gave Jesus a piece of broiled fish, and Jesus took it and ate it in their presence.

Jesus said to the disciples, "This is what I told you while I was still with you: Everything must be fulfilled that is written about me. This is what is written: The Christ will suffer and rise from the dead on the third day. Repentance and forgiveness of sins will be preached in his name to all nations. You are witnesses of these things."

One of the disciples named Thomas was not present that night. The others told Thomas they had seen Jesus. But he did not believe. Thomas said that he would only believe if he could see and feel the wounds in Jesus' hands and feet and side.

The next week when the disciples were again gathered and Thomas was present, Jesus appeared again. Jesus said, "Peace be with you." Then Jesus said to Thomas, "Put your finger here; see my hands. Reach out your hand and put it into the wound in my side. Stop doubting and believe."

Thomas said to Jesus, "My Lord and my God!"

Then Jesus told Thomas, "Because you have seen me, you have believed; blessed are those who have not seen and yet have believed."

Food for Thought:

1. Remember in an earlier story that Jesus told his disciples he would be killed but would be raised to life on the third day. This happened just as Jesus said would happen.
2. Why were the two men walking on the road so sad?
3. What did Jesus tell the men? Did the men recognize Jesus while they walked and talked?
4. What happened when Jesus sat down to eat with the men and blessed and broke the bread?
5. What did the men do?
6. When Jesus appeared in the room with the disciples, what did they think they were seeing?

7. What did Jesus ask for? And what did he do with it in their presence?
8. What did Thomas say when the disciples said they had seen Jesus?
9. When Jesus appeared with the disciples again and Thomas was there, what did Jesus say to Thomas?
10. If the listeners had been there, would they be like Thomas who needed to see Jesus, or would they believe without seeing Jesus?
11. Do listeners believe that Jesus is indeed alive today?

Food for the Heart: "Though you have not seen him, you love him; and even though you do not see him now, you believe in him and are filled with…. joy, for you are receiving the goal of your faith, the salvation of your souls" (1 Pet.1:8-9).

36. Breakfast on the Beach

Scripture Base: John 21:1-18

Prepare the Food:

1. Have any listeners ever denied knowing someone because of fear? Or perhaps they kept quiet when they should have spoken out?
2. When something like this happens there could be hard feelings, even anger, or disappointment. How can one make it right? Who must be the first to restore the broken relationship?

Serve the Meal:

Breakfast on the Beach

Before Jesus was arrested he warned the disciple Simon Peter that he would deny knowing Jesus three times. It happened just as Jesus said after Jesus was arrested and Simon Peter denied him. After Jesus' death and resurrection Jesus appeared to his disciples one morning while they were fishing. Simon Peter and two other disciples were in the boat fishing all night but they caught nothing.

Early in the morning, Jesus stood on the shore, but the disciples did not realize that it was Jesus. He called out to the disciples, "Friends, have you caught any fish?"

"No," they answered.

Jesus replied, "Throw your net on the right side of the boat and you will find some." When the disciples did as Jesus instructed, they were unable to haul the net in because of the large number of fish.

Then the disciple named John said to Simon Peter, "It is the Lord!" As soon as Simon Peter heard John's words, "It is the Lord," he wrapped his outer garment around him and jumped into the water. The other disciples followed in the boat, towing the net full of fish, for they were not far from the shore. When the disciples arrived at the shore, they saw a fire of burning coals with some fish cooking on it, and some bread.

Jesus said to the disciples, "Bring some of the fish you have just caught."

Simon Peter climbed into the boat to drag the net full of large fish ashore.

Jesus said to the disciples, "Come and have breakfast." None of the disciples dared to ask him, "Who are you?" They knew it was the Lord. Jesus took the bread and gave it to the disciples. He did the same with the fish he was cooking. This was now the third time Jesus appeared to his disciples after he was raised from the dead.

When they had finished eating, Jesus said to Simon Peter, "Simon, son of John, do you truly love me more than these?"

Yes, Lord, you know that I love you," Simon Peter replied.

Jesus said, "Feed my lambs." Again Jesus said, "Simon, son of John, do you truly love me?"

Simon Peter answered, "Yes, Lord, you know that I love you."

Jesus said, "Take care of my sheep." The third time Jesus said to Simon Peter, "Simon, son of John, do you love me?"

Simon Peter was hurt because Jesus asked him the third time, "Do you love me?" So he said, "Lord, you know all things; you know that I love you."

Jesus said, "Feed my sheep. I tell you the truth, when you were younger you dressed yourself and went where you wanted; but when you are old you will stretch out your hands, and someone else will dress you and lead you where you do not want to go." Jesus said this to show what kind of death by which Simon Peter would glorify God. Then Jesus said to Simon Peter, "Follow me!"

Food for Thought:

1. What did Jesus tell Simon Peter that he was going to do?
2. Do listeners think that Simon Peter believed Jesus that this would actually happen?
3. Read to the listeners Mark 14:66-72.

4. Each time what did Simon Peter say when asked if he knew Jesus?
5. After the resurrection some of the disciples who were fishermen returned to their fishing. Had they caught anything during the night?
6. What did Jesus tell the disciples to do? Did they obey? What happened when they obeyed?
7. What was Jesus doing on the shore? What food was he cooking for the disciples?
8. When they finished eating, what did Jesus ask Simon Peter?
9. What did Simon Peter reply?
10. Why do you think that Jesus asked Simon Peter three times if he loved Jesus? How many times did Simon Peter deny knowing Jesus?
11. Did Jesus love Simon Peter?
12. Do listeners think that Simon Peter truly loved Jesus?
13. If we become believers in Jesus, what should we be careful not to do? (deny Jesus)
14. Do the listeners love Jesus? Talk about how they can show they love Jesus.

Food for the Heart: "Whosoever therefore shall confess me before men, him will I confess also before my Father which is in heaven.

But whosoever shall deny me before men, him will I also deny before my Father which is in heaven" (Matt. 10:32-33 KJV).

37. The Believers Broke Bread Together

Scripture Base: Acts 2:42; 16:34

Prepare the Food:

1. When Jesus returned to heaven there were two things the followers of Jesus might do. They could give up and go back to their old ways because their leader was gone. Or they could come together and obey what their leader Jesus commanded them to do.
2. In this story you will see that the believers did come together and began to share with one another and eat together in fellowship as though Jesus were still with them.

Serve the Meal:

The Believers Broke Bread Together

After Jesus returned to heaven a time came when God sent his Holy Spirit to anoint the followers of Jesus. They were gathered in one place when suddenly the sound like a violent blowing wind came from heaven and they saw what appeared to be tongues of fire that came to rest on each one. All of the followers were filled with God's Holy Spirit.

Simon Peter stood before a crowd and gave his testimony about Jesus. He told the people, "After Jesus was put to death he was raised to life again and there were many witnesses that Jesus was indeed alive. When Jesus returned to heaven he was exalted (honored) to sit at the right hand of God the Father. Then God made this Jesus, who was crucified, both Lord and Christ."

When the people heard these words they were cut to the heart and said to Simon Peter, "Brothers, what shall we do?"

Simon Peter replied, "Repent and be baptized, everyone of you, in the name of Jesus Christ so that you may be forgiven. And you will receive the gift of the Holy Spirit." Those who accepted Simon Peter's message were baptized; about three thousand were added to the followers of Jesus that day.

The followers of Jesus devoted themselves to the teaching of the disciples who taught the people as Jesus taught them. The believers gathered in fellowship and in the breaking of bread together and prayer. All the believers were together and shared everything in common. Every day they continued to meet together in the temple courts. They broke bread in their homes and ate together with glad and sincere hearts. They praised God and enjoyed the favor of all the people. And God continued to add new believers who were being saved to their number every day.

Food for Thought:

1. After Jesus returned to heaven and the believers were gathered together, what happened? What do listeners think this means?
2. What happened when Simon Peter told the people about Jesus? What did the people say?
3. What did Simon Peter tell the people to do?
4. What were the believers doing from day to day? What do listeners think "breaking bread" means? (sharing their bread as they ate)
5. Were the believers happy together? How did they show their happiness?
6. Do listeners think that God was pleased with what the believers were doing? How did God show his pleasure? (added to their number)

Food for the Heart: "The word is near you; it is in your mouth and in your heart: That if you confess with your mouth 'Jesus is Lord,' and believe in your heart that God raised him from the dead, you will be saved. For it is with your heart that you believe...and it is with your mouth you confess and are saved" (Rom. 10:8-10)

38. Peter's Strange Dream About Food

Scripture Base: Acts 10:1-48; 11:1-18

Prepare the Food:

1. Briefly explain about the foods that God told the people not to eat because they were to be a holy people—set apart from other peoples. (see Lev. 11:1-47 & Deut. 14:3-20)
2. Are there certain foods that listeners do not eat or believe to be unclean?
3. Are there certain people that listeners believe to be impure or unclean?
4. The descendants of Abraham (Jews) considered the places where non-Jews lived to be unclean and they would not eat with them because of this.
5. Say that God sometimes speaks to us through dreams to prepare us to serve Him. In today's story an angel appeared to tell what a man named Cornelius was to do and a vision told Simon Peter what he was to do.

Serve the Meal:

Peter's Strange Dream About Food

When the descendants of Abraham left Egypt, God gave the people a list of foods they were not to eat. This was because God wanted to set the people apart from others and to test their obedience. Through the years the people did not eat those foods and considered them unclean.

There was a foreign soldier named Cornelius who feared God and gave to those in need and prayed regularly. One day an angel appeared to Cornelius and told him that God heard his prayers and saw his gifts to the poor. Then the angel told Cornelius to send for a man named Simon Peter. So Cornelius sent two of his servants and a soldier to get Simon Peter.

About noon the next day the men were approaching the house where Simon Peter was staying. Simon Peter had gone up on the roof to pray. There he became hungry and wanted something to eat. While the food was being prepared, Simon Peter fell into a trance. He saw heaven opened and something like a large sheet was let down to earth by its four corners. In the sheet were all kinds of four-footed animals, as well as reptiles and birds. Then a voice told Simon Peter, "Get up. Kill and eat."

"Surely not, Lord!" Peter replied. "I have never eaten anything impure or unclean."

The voice spoke to Simon Peter a second time, "Do not call anything impure that God has made clean."

This happened three times, and immediately the sheet was taken back into heaven. While Simon Peter was wondering about the meaning of the vision, the men sent by Cornelius arrived and called out for Simon Peter. While he was still thinking about the vision, the Holy Spirit said to Simon Peter, "Three men are looking for you. Do not hesitate to go with them, for I have sent them."

The men told why they had come, so Simon Peter invited them into the house to be his guests. The next day Simon Peter went with the men and arrived at the house of Cornelius the following day. Cornelius was expecting them. As Simon Peter entered the house, Cornelius met him and fell at his feet in reverence. But Simon Peter made Cornelius get up. "I'm only a man," Simon Peter said to Cornelius.

Simon Peter went inside the house and found a large gathering of people. He said to them, "You are well aware that it is against our law for a Jew to associate with those who are not Jewish. But God has shown me that I should not call any man impure or unclean."

Then Cornelius told about the angel that had appeared to him and how the angel said to send for Simon Peter. Then Cornelius said, "Now we are all here in the presence of God to listen to everything the Lord has commanded you to tell us."

Then Simon Peter began to speak, "God does not show favoritism, but accepts men from every nation who fear him and do what is right. This is the message God sent to the descendants of Abraham telling the good news of peace through Jesus Christ." Then Simon Peter told what had happened to Jesus and how he was put to death and then raised again. And he said that all the prophets testified about Jesus that everyone who believes in Jesus receives forgiveness of sins through his name.

While Simon Peter was still speaking these words the Holy Spirit was poured out on those hearing the message. Then Simon Peter said, "Can anyone keep these people from being baptized with water? They have received the Holy Spirit just as we have." So Simon Peter ordered that the entire household be baptized in the name of Jesus Christ. Afterward Simon Peter stayed with the household of Cornelius a few days.

Later Simon Peter had to explain to other believers why he went into the house of uncircumcised believers and ate with them. He explained that God had given the household of Cornelius the same gift of the Holy Spirit because they, too, believed in Christ. When the others heard these words, they had no further objections and even began to praise God who granted these foreigners repentance unto life.

Food for Thought:
1. How did God prepare Simon Peter for what God wanted him to do?
2. What did Simon Peter say when the voice said, "Kill and eat."
3. As soon as Simon Peter's vision ended who arrived?
4. Did Simon Peter welcome the foreigners to come into his house?
5. When Simon Peter went to the house of Cornelius did he go in?
6. What did Simon Peter tell the people who were gathered inside?
7. What happened while Simon Peter was still speaking?

8. What did this tell Simon Peter? Do listeners think that now Simon Peter understood what God was telling him?
9. When Simon Peter saw what was happening what did he order to happen?
10. Later what did Simon Peter need to explain to the other leaders?
11. Did they understand?
12. In those days the people who were not descendants of Abraham (Jews) were called Gentiles. Before Jesus returned to heaven he told his disciples: "Go and make disciples of all nations, and baptize them in the name of God the Father, Jesus the Son and the Holy Spirit and to teach them to obey everything that Jesus commanded. "All nations" includes all of us who are Gentiles. God loves all people and wants all to share in the forgiveness of sin. Our sin makes us "unclean" and "impure." But Jesus shed his blood as a sacrifice to make us clean in God's sight. A prophet named Isaiah wrote:

> "Come now, let us reason together," says the LORD. Though your sins be as scarlet, they shall be as white as snow; though the are red like crimson, they shall be like wool" (Isa. 1:18).

Food for the Heart: "The Spirit clearly says that in later times some will abandon the faith and follow deceiving spirits and things taught by demons....They forbid people to marry and order them to abstain from certain foods, which God created to be received with thanksgiving, because it is consecrated by the word of God and prayer" (1 Tim. 4:1, 3-4).

Note: The point of this story is less about food than it is about obeying what God tells us to do, and about the barriers that God has broken down so we can hear the Good News and can share it with others so they can be made clean and pure in God's presence also.

39. Eating Food Offered to Idols

Scripture Base: 1 Corinthians 8:1-11
Prepare the Food:
1. What things might listeners do that would influence others either for good or for bad?
2. When God forgives our sins and makes us clean, are we then free to do anything we want to do, whether it is good for us or bad for others? (set a bad example, or give a bad testimony about who we are)

Serve the Meal:

Eating Food Offered to Idols

In the days of the teacher named Paul there were people who believed that a person could do anything, good or bad, because it didn't matter since our bodies are evil and our spirits are pure. Others who were believers in Jesus needed to understand that their actions, even if not harmful to them, could have harmful influence on those who were not believers.

There were new believers that Paul told about Jesus. They believed in Jesus just like Paul. But they had questions about what was right or good to do. So Paul wrote a letter teaching them what was right and best for them and for others who lived among them.

Paul wrote: "Now about food offered to idols: We know that we all possess knowledge and that knowledge can cause us to be puffed up. Love is better because it builds up. So then, about eating food sacrificed to idols: We know that an idol is nothing at all in the world. And there is only one God. Even if there were many so-called gods, whether in heaven or on earth, we know there is only one true God for us. He is the Father from whom all things come and for whom we live. And there is one Lord Jesus Christ through whom all things came and through whom we live.

But not everyone knows this. Some people are so accustomed to idols that when they eat such food they think of it as sacrificed to an idol because their conscience is weak, it is defiled. But food does not bring us near to God; we are no worse if we do not eat, and no better if we do.

Be careful, however, that the exercise of your freedom does not become a stumbling block to the weak. For if anyone with a weak conscience sees you who have this knowledge eating in an idol's temple, then he may be encouraged to eat what has been sacrificed to idols. So this weak brother, for whom Christ died, is destroyed by your knowledge. When you sin against our brothers in this way and wound their weak conscience, you sin against Christ.

Therefore, if what I eat causes my brother to fall into sin, I will never eat meat again, so that I will not cause my brother to fall."

Food for Thought:
1. If idols are not true gods, then what might be wrong with eating food offered to idols?
2. When we become believers in Jesus Christ as Savior, could there be some things from the old way of life that we would no longer want to do?
3. If eating food that has been sacrificed to idols causes those with a weak conscience (weak faith and understanding) to stumble, would we want to continue doing it?
4. Are there some other things that might cause a weaker brother or sister to stumble and doubt?

Food for the Heart: "So whether you eat or drink or whatever you do, do it all for the glory of God. Do not cause anyone to stumble....For I am not seeking my own good but the good of many, so that they may be saved" (1 Cor. 10:31, 32a, 33b)

40. Eating Worthily at The Lord's Table

Scripture Base: Luke 22:14-20; 1 Corinthians 11:17-34

Prepare the Food:

1. The memorial meal that Christians eat together remembers the death of Jesus for our sins. It also looks back to the time during the days of Moses when God told the people to sprinkle blood on their doorways and to eat a Passover Meal because God's angel of judgment was going to pass over their homes and harm no one.₁
2. It is also a time to examine our hearts so that we eat worthily at the Lord's Table. Here is the story.

Serve the Meal:

Eating Worthily at The Lord's Table

When Jesus ate the Last Supper with his disciples, he took bread, gave thanks and broke it and gave it to his disciples saying, "This is my body given for you; do this in remembrance of me."

The same way Jesus took the cup and said, "This cup is the new covenant in my blood, which is poured out for you."

After Jesus returned to heaven, those who believed in Jesus continued to honor Jesus by eating this meal together. But some in the new churches did not honor Jesus by what they did. This happened in the church at Corinth. The teacher Paul wrote a letter warning the people:

"I hear that when you come together there are divisions among you....When you come together, it is not the Lord's Supper you eat, for as you eat, each of you goes ahead without waiting for anybody else. One remains hungry, another gets drunk. Don't you have homes to eat in? Or do you despise God's people and humiliate those who have nothing? What shall I say to you?

For I received from the Lord what I also passed on to you: The Lord Jesus, on the night he was betrayed took bread, and when he had given thanks, he broke it and said, 'This is my body which is for you; do this in remembrance of me.' In the same way, Jesus took the cup, saying, 'This is the new covenant in my blood; whenever you drink it, do this in remembrance of me.' For whenever you eat this bread and drink this cup, you proclaim the Lord's death until he comes.

Therefore, whoever eats the bread or drinks the cup of the Lord in an unworthy manner will be guilty of sinning against the body and blood of the Lord. A man ought to examine himself before he eats of the bread and drinks of the cup. For anyone who eats and drinks without recognizing the body of the Lord eats and drinks judgment on himself.

So then, my brothers, when you come together to eat, wait for each other. If anyone is hungry, he should eat at home, so that when you meet together it may not result in judgment."

Food for Thought:
1. Recall in an earlier story that Jesus said he was he bread come down from heaven. What do listeners think Jesus meant by his words when he broke the bread and said, "This is my body."
2. Could it be this was a picture to remind believers that Jesus was put to death (his body broken) for our sins?
3. What about the cup? Could it be that Jesus was letting this represent his blood that was shed for our sins?
4. Why do believers in Jesus eat this meal together? (To remember Jesus and to proclaim our Lord's death until he returns for us)
5. Why should believers be careful to examine their hearts before eating the meal? Should believers be careful how they eat the meal with others?
6. If the meal is eaten unworthily who judges the person?

Food for the Heart: "Therefore, whoever eats the bread or drinks the cup of the Lord in an unworthy manner will be guilty of sinning against the body and blood of the Lord" (1 Cor. 11:27).

41. Meat or Milk?

Scripture Base: 1 Corinthians 3:2; Hebrews 5:11-14; 6:1, 4-6; 1 Peter 2:2

Prepare the Food:
1. What kind of food do listeners give to a newborn baby? Do they give meat like they eat, or do they provide milk for the baby?
2. When listeners teach children, do they teach the difficult things first, or do they begin with the easier things the children can understand?
3. What do new believers in Jesus need—teaching that is difficult to digest like meat, or teaching that is like milk—easy to digest (or understand)?

Serve the Meal:

Meat or Milk?

In the Bible the person who wrote the Book of Hebrews was writing a letter to believers to warn them about falling away—that is, leaving Jesus and going back to the old religion and way of life. He wrote these words:

> We have much to say about this, but it is hard to explain because you are slow to learn. In fact, by this time you ought to be teachers, but you are the ones who need someone to teach you the elementary truths of God's Word all over again.

> You need milk, not solid food! Anyone who lives on milk, being still an infant, is not acquainted with the teaching about righteousness. But solid food is for the mature, who by constant use have trained themselves to distinguish good from evil (Heb. 5:11-14).

> So let us leave the elementary teachings about Christ and go on to maturity....It is impossible for those who have tasted the heavenly gift, who have shared in the Holy Spirit, who have tasted the goodness of the word of God to be brought back to repentance if they fall away. Because it means cru-

cifying the Son of God all over again and subjecting Christ to public disgrace (Heb. 6:1, 4-6).

The teacher Paul wrote to some friends who had divisions among them in their church. He said:

> Brothers, I could not address you as spiritual but as worldly—mere infants in Christ. I gave you milk, not solid food, for you were not yet ready for it, Indeed, you are still not ready. You are still worldly. For since there is jealousy and quarreling among you, are you not worldly? Are you not acting like mere men (1 Cor. 3:1-3)?
>
> I am not writing this to shame you, but to warn you, as my dear children (1 Cor. 4:14).

The disciple Simon Peter wrote in a letter:

> Therefore rid yourselves of all malice and all deceit, hypocrisy, envy, and slander of every kind. Like newborn babies, crave pure spiritual milk, so that by it you may grow up in your salvation, now that you have tasted that the Lord is good (1 Pet. 2:1-3).

Food for Thought:

1. Were these people as believers mature or were they behaving like infants who needed simple spiritual food?
2. In our lives as followers of Jesus we must put aside everything that is not good and desire that which is best and honors Jesus.
3. As we grow we can handle the mature spiritual food—real meat—and understand it and live by it.
4. So we ask ourselves: Are we ready for real spiritual food or do we still need milk as infants in Christ?

Food for the Heart: "The righteous eat to their hearts' content, but the stomach of the wicked goes hungry" (Prov. 13:25).

42. Full Bellies and Starving Souls

Scripture Base: Deuteronomy 8:3; Matthew 25:31, 34-46; John 6:14-15, 25-27, 33, 35

Prepare the Food:
1. The Bible warns against gluttony—eating more than we need and hoarding food that could be eaten by others.
2. The Bible also warns about not sharing with those in need who long for the scraps that fall from our tables. Recall the story of The Rich Fool (Luke 12:15-21).

Serve the Meal:

Full Bellies and Starving Souls

When Satan tempted Jesus to turn stones into bread—to fill his belly—Jesus said to Satan: "Man does not live by bread alone, but by every word that comes from the mouth of God."

After Jesus fed the 5,000 men, plus women and children, and the people saw this miraculous sign that Jesus did, they began to say, "Surely this is the Prophet who is to come into the world." Jesus knew the people were intending to come and make him king by force, so he went away by himself into the hills.

When the people found Jesus later he said to them, "I tell you the truth, you are looking for me, not because you saw miraculous signs but because you ate the loaves and had your fill. Do not work for food that spoils, but for food that endures to eternal life." Then Jesus reminded the people that he is the bread come down from heaven and gives life to the world. Jesus declared, "….He who comes to me will never go hungry…"

When the Son of Man comes in his glory, and all the angels with him, he will sit on his throne in heavenly glory. Then the King will say to those on his right, "Come, you who are blessed by my Father; take your inheritance, the kingdom prepared for you since the creation of the world. For I was hungry and you gave me something to eat. I was thirsty and you gave me something to drink, I was a stranger and you invited me in. I needed clothes and you clothed me, I was sick and you looked after me, I was in prison and you came to visit me."

Then the righteous will answer him, "Lord, when did we see you hungry and feed you, or thirsty and give you something to drink? When did we see you a stranger and invite you in, or needing clothes and clothe you? When did we see you sick or in prison and go visit you?"

The King will reply, "I tell you the truth, whatever you did for the least of these brothers of mine, you did for me." Then he will say to those on his left, "Depart from me, you who are cursed, into the eternal fire prepared for the devil and his angels. For I was hungry and you gave me nothing to eat, I was thirsty and you gave me nothing to drink. I was a stranger and you did not invite me in, I needed clothes and you did not clothe me, I was sick and in prison and you did not visit me."

They will answer, "Lord, when did we see you hungry or thirsty or a stranger or needing clothes or sick or in prison, and did not help you?"

He will reply, "I tell you the truth, whatever you did not do for one of the least of these, you did not do for me."

Food for Thought:

1. What did Jesus consider most important: Feeding on God's Word or turning some stones into bread?
2. Who provides the true bread that satisfies the spirit?
3. Why is it important to share one's food with others? Who might you be feeding?
4. Which is better for your soul, feeding on God's Word or selfishly enjoying gluttony of food others may need?

Food for the Heart: "Listen, my son, and be wise, and keep your heart on the right path. Do not join those who drink too much wine or gorge themselves on meat, for drunkards and gluttons become poor, and drowsiness clothes them in rags" (Prov. 23:19-21).

43. Tree of Life Bearing Fruit For Life and Healing

Scripture Base: Genesis 2:9; 3:22; Psalm 1; Ezekiel 47:7, 12; Revelation 2:7; 23:1-3

Prepare the Food:

1. Remember the tree of life mentioned in the story of Adam and Eve? What happened after Adam and Eve disobeyed God? Could they still eat from the tree of life?
2. Do listeners know of a tree whose fruit gives life and whose leaves are for healing?

Serve the Meal:

Tree of Life Bearing Fruit For Life and Healing

In the story of Adam and Eve, after they disobeyed God by eating from the tree of the knowledge of good and evil, God banished them from the garden where the tree of life grew. An angel with a flaming sword was placed at the entrance to the tree of life so Adam and Eve could no longer eat from it and live forever.

A prophet named Ezekiel had a vision. In his vision he saw a river flowing with a great number of trees on each side of the river. The river was filled with life and wherever the river flowed everything will live. The trees were fruit trees of all kinds growing on both banks of the river. The leaves of the trees will not wither, and the fruit will not fail. Every month the trees will bear fruit. The fruit will serve as food and the leaves for healing (Ezek. 47:7, 9, 12).

The disciple named John also had a vision of the End Times.

Following the judgment and punishment of Satan and his demons and all those who rejected Jesus as God's Son and Savior, a time of great blessing will come. John also saw a river of water clear as crystal flowing from the throne of God.

On each side of the river stood the tree of life, bearing twelve crops of fruit. Each month the trees were bearing fruit. The leaves of the trees are for healing of the nations. No longer will there be any curse. The throne of God and of the Lamb—Jesus—will be there. Paradise like what Adam and Eve knew in the Garden of Eden will be restored. There will be no angel with a flaming sword to block the way to the tree of life (Rev. 22:1-3).

In John's vision Jesus the Lamb of God spoke to him with words to the seven churches. He said, "To him who overcomes, I will give the right to eat from the tree of life, which is in the paradise of God." (Rev. 2:7)

Food for Thought:
1. This story has parts of a continuing story in it. The story reminds us that God is preparing a pleasant place for those who believe in Jesus and whose sins are forgiven.
2. It is a picture of abundant food each month and all year long as the trees bear their fruit.
3. The leaves are for the healing of the nations. People will live in harmony and peace. There will be no more war and suffering.
4. The trees grow along the river coming from the throne of God. It is God who provides our food and water and who has provided forgiveness of sin and everlasting life through his Son Jesus, our Savior.
5. The tree of life will be part of the great blessing awaiting those who confess their sins, repent from sinning, believe in Jesus and accept his forgiveness. God's Word says this and God's Word can be trusted.

Food for the Heart: "To him who overcomes, I will give the right to eat from the tree of life, which is in the paradise of God" (Rev. 2:7).

44. A Place at the Table Saved for You

Scripture Base: Isaiah 25:6; Matthew 22:2-14; Luke 22:27-30

Prepare the Food:

1. These stories tell about a feast—a place at the table—for those who have been invited. The stories remind us that many have been invited to come and eat, but some have refused.
2. All are invited to come. One accepts the invitation by believing in Jesus as God's Son who suffered and died for our sins.

Serve the Meal:

A Place at the Table Saved for You

Do you remember the time a man said to Jesus, "Blessed is the man who will eat at the feast in the kingdom of God?" Jesus then told the story about the man who prepared a great feast and sent out invitations for many guests. At the time when the feast was ready, the man sent his servants to call the guests to come and eat. But the guests instead made excuses and did not come. So the man sent his servant to invite others who were poor, crippled, or blind. When there was more room at his table, the man sent the servant to compel others to come also so that his table might be filled.

There is another story like this one. Jesus said the kingdom of heaven is like a king who prepared a wedding feast for his son. The king sent his servants to those who had been invited to tell them to come, but they refused to come. Then the king sent some more servants to tell those invited that the food was prepared—Come to the wedding feast. But the invited guests paid no attention. Some guests even seized the king's servants, mistreated them and killed them. The king was very angry. So he sent his army to punish those guests. Then the king told his servants, "The wedding feast is ready, but those I invited did not come. Go out and invite to the feast anyone you can find." So the servants obeyed the king and soon the wedding hall was filled with guests. But when the king came in to see the guests, he noticed a man there who was not wearing wedding clothes. "Friend," the king asked, "how did you get in here without wedding clothes?" The man was speechless. Then the king told his servants, "Tie him hand and foot, and throw him outside, into the darkness, where there will be weeping and gnashing of teeth." (Matt. 22:2-14)

Then Jesus said, "For many are invited, but few are chosen."

At another time Jesus asked his disciples: "Who is greater, the one who sits at the table or the one who serves? Is it not the one who sits at the table? But I am among you as one who serves. You are those who have stood by me in my trials. And I confer on you a kingdom....so that you may eat and drink at my table in my kingdom..." (Luke 22:27-30

A writer in the book about the last days wrote: "Then the angel said to me, 'Write: Blessed are those who are invited to the wedding supper of the Lamb!'" And he added, "These are the true words of God." (Rev. 19:9)

Food for Thought:
1. What did the man tell Jesus about those who will eat at the feast in the kingdom of God?
2. Have the listeners ever heard of such a thing as invited guests refusing to come to a feast prepared for them?
3. These stories are telling about the preparations that God is making for those who believe in Jesus as Savior. A place at the table means that there will be fellowship with Jesus and with other believers.
4. The man who was not wearing wedding clothes is a man who was not a believer clothed in Jesus' righteousness.

Food for the Heart: "On this mountain the LORD Almighty will prepare a feast of rich food for all peoples..." (Isa. 25:66).

Guidelines for Bible Storying

Selecting the Bible Stories

The following pages contain helpful information for you if are not familiar with developing your own sets of Bible stories and lessons, are not experienced in telling the stories, and leading a learning time. This same information is available in an expanded form in *Basic Bible Storying* from www.churchstarting.net.

Selecting Stories to Tell

The Bible stories in this book were selected primarily for telling during disaster response or famine relief ministries. Their theme is generally food or eating. However, these stories may be mixed with other stories like *The Water Stories*, *The Grief Stories*, or *The Hope Stories*[5]. There is overlap with some of these same stories used in these sets as well, though the food theme may not be emphasized.

I have included an increasing evangelistic theme development toward the last stories. Feel free to make the stories as "evangelistic" as your listeners will accept. Since the stories might be used among people who are not yet that open to the Gospel, I have begun more food-centered theme in the early stories.

These Stories are a Suggested Resource

You will probably not need all of these stories or not have time to tell all of them. You will, therefore, select the ones most likely to be interesting or appropriate for your listeners. Feel free to add other stories that you feel are needed to prepare or transition to these stories.

Not an Oral Bible. Also let me say here that I was not attempting to provide an *Oral Bible* that generally requires stories closer to the verbatim. I have taken some liberties by compiling a narrative from several Bible references to build a theme-based story. If you are not comfortable using these compiled stories which do use Scripture, then skip over these or adapt them for your needs.

The pre-story introductory questions and discussion are labeled *Prepare the Food*. And the post-story questions and discussion are labeled as *Food for Thought*. These labels are not for sharing, only for delineating the parts of a story session. It may be that according to time or other circumstances all one can do is tell the Bible stories without any pre or post-story introduction or discussion. This is fine. But if there is opportunity to do more, then by all means be prepared to take advantage of the moment for appropriate teaching and learning.

Primary theme of food, hunger, eating or preparing food. In some stories the matter of eating or food is not necessarily central but more peripheral. Some stories related to eating I have deliberately left out as they introduced themes that needed more introduction or preceding and following stories to properly frame them and give proper meaning.

The story of Lot's providing unleavened bread for the two angels when they came to Sodom to warn Lot is an example. The prohibition about eating blood was mentioned in the Flood Story but not explored in any depth. This prohibition raises problems in some cultures and may bring up issues you would then need to stop and deal with.

Some stories have only implied eating or food so have not been used. One example is the story of Jesus in the home of Mary and Martha in Luke 10 where Martha comes from preparing food to ask that Mary be urged to help her. No doubt the story of the 2,000 pigs that perished when the evil spirits entered them would cause rejoicing among Muslims and horror among those where the pig is a staple meat. I have also been among people who have gladly eaten the serpent in the Garden of Eden! We must remember that feelings about different foods vary among differing peoples and plan our stories that deal with food to accommodate and respect the exact feelings of the listeners so they won't reject the story and miss the central truth the story teaches.

Where to Begin

Begin by selecting the stories that are most appropriate for your listeners, or the occasions that you will have for telling the stories. You may prepare an exact number that you plan to tell, or prepare a few extra just in case you need more.

1. Select an appropriate number of stories to tell to fit the time with your listeners. If pre-evangelism or evangelism are objectives, you might want to plan backwards from the last more-evangelistic stories toward the first attention-getting food stories.
2. Prioritize the stories that are "must tell," "should tell," or "might tell," if time permits.
3. Be aware of general worldview issues of audience concerning food and eating that might affect the story choice or the listeners' interest and acceptance of the story. This is not to say "Don't offend" but to say that it is important to keep listeners interested and willing to hear more until all stories are heard. We call this keeping our storying "win/win" until the finish.

Preparing the Bible Stories

Read the Scripture Base Passages

The Scripture Base references are the ones I would use to get a perspective and a theme development. You will note in some instances I have included several parallel accounts from which I compiled the stories for telling. This was my choice but it does not need to be yours. After several readings aloud you should begin to hear a story emerging. I have suggested reading the passages aloud. You hear the passages differently when read aloud as opposed to silent reading. Also this will begin to give you a feeling of how the story will sound as you tell it.

Make a List of Any Additional Passages or Parts to the Stories

Since you will be the storyteller, you are free to make any changes that you feel are needed. I have mostly used the *New International Version* for my stories but have taken some liberties in how I expressed things in the stories, so the wording is not exactly the same. When you have decided on what to include in your stories, then you are ready for the next step.

Write Out the Story as You Plan to Tell It

Because we are literates, we usually feel more comfortable if we write out what we plan to say or tell. I have written out the stories in this model resource in order to share my ideas about what stories to tell and how to tell the stories. After you have been telling the Bible stories for a time, you may reach a point where you no longer need to write out each story you plan to tell. Over time I learned many of these stories and so have a library of learned stories to pick and choose from when telling Bible stories.

1. Adapt the stories for telling as stories and not as lectures. Some stories may reflect more of narrative ac-

count than a typical story with characters, plot and location, but keep it as "story" as possible.
2. Do you need to introduce a story or give background so listeners will be prepared to understand any unfamiliar things in the story?
3. Think about what other audience preparation is needed for hearing a Bible story and understanding or relating to it?

Considerations for Crafting (Oralizing) Bible Stories for Telling

Shorten Long Stories

Shorter stories are both easier to tell by the storyer and easier to remember for the storyer and the listeners. Longer and more complex stories may need shortening. One way to make a decision on this is to read the story a number of times and then retell it and see what you naturally leave in the story and what you leave out. A general guideline is to limit proper names and places to around three.

Keep Unusual Features

Repetition of certain story phrases or items in the Bible account are important in the theme of the story as it provides emphasis to certain key truths or ties the story parts together as a developing theme. For example, in the Flood Story, three times the biblical story says that Noah did everything that God commanded. Important matters, such as this affirmation, may be important in the story you are telling and its theme development.

Stereotype Characters to Prevent Confusion.

You attain the meaning of this suggestion by attaching a descriptive term to certain names to help listeners keep them straight. A common illustration is that of Ehud, the left-handed, and Eglon, the fat, in Judges 3. In the preceding stories I chose to call Peter by his longer name "Simon Peter" rather than toggling back and forth as the stories do in calling him Simon or Peter or Simon Peter. I also chose to call the Israelites the "descendants of Abraham" which raises less of a red flag with many Islamic listeners. Decide whether to use "Lord" or "God" for consistency.

Among many oral listeners titles are helpful and perhaps even needed when referring to important characters. I have tried to be consistent in saying "King Saul" or "Prophet Elijah." I did however, refer to Pharaoh as King of Egypt rather than Pharaoh since "king" is generally understood by most listeners.

The Importance of Character Dialog

Character dialog makes the stories more complicated to remember and tell, but it also makes the stories far more interesting and less of being just a descriptive narrative of what happened. Dialog also slows the stories down. To speed some stories along it can be helpful just to narrate what the characters said and keep only the essential or dramatic character dialog.

Also in using the dialog it is often less confusing to interpreters and listeners if the storyer will identify who is speaking to whom, and then continue the dialog without breaking it as is commonly done in written translations to make the reading a bit more interesting for literates.

Example: "Be careful," Jesus warned them, "Watch out for the yeast of the Pharisees and that of Herod" Mark. 8:15.

Jesus warned his disciples, "Be careful. Watch out for the yeast of the Pharisees and that of Herod. (speaker and listeners identified and dialog uninterrupted.)

It is generally helpful to replace pronouns as used in the Bible versions with proper names to avoid confusion. Some pronouns can be used where the pronoun is used close to the person(s) referred to. Avoid uses of multiple pronouns without identifying who is referred to. *Ex*: The Pharisees and all the Jews do not eat unless *they* give their hands a ceremonial washing...When *they* come from the marketplace *they* do not eat unless they wash. And *they* observe many other traditions...(Mark 7:3-4).

That story continues and in verse 9 it says: "And he said to them..." It would be better to say instead: "And *Jesus* said to the *Pharisees and teachers of the law*..."

Doing this helps you the storyteller to better visualize who is speaking to whom as you tell the stories. And it helps your listeners to follow the characters' dialog as you tell the story.

For more information and suggestions for crafting or oralizing Bible stories for telling see *Basic Bible Storying*.[6]

Telling the Bible Stories

Learning the Bible Stories

Repetition is the key to learning. Read the story aloud several times, first to get the overall flow of the story, and each succeeding time to see the story visually and to add emphasis and pacing for telling. Then tell the story or as much of it as you can remember. Longer stories may still require either outlined notes or reading with as much eye contact as possible and gestures as appropriate.

Telling Through an Interpreter

When it is necessary to work through an interpreter, several things are helpful.

- First, go over the story(ies) with the interpreter so there are no surprises and no terms to come up suddenly that need some thought or clarification.

- Second, provide the interpreter a copy of the written story itself—just the story and perhaps in larger font (like 14) for easy readability.

- Third, think ahead to be sure to give the interpreter a subject and verb and story narration that is uncomplicated grammatically. Interpreters need complete phrases, but not too lengthy.

Telling the Stories

If pre-story discussion, review or introduction is used first, then it is helpful to make a transition by saying, "Now here is the story from the Bible." If you will hold a Bible, then open it at the "story" and begin telling the story. At the conclusion of the story say, "That ends the story from the Bible." Close the Bible or put it down to signal that the story itself is finished.

Stories should be told as far as possible as *stories* with characters, location (if important), plot, and character dialog. A narrated story where the storyer just tells the story as a third person witness is usually simpler and faster to tell but less engaging. If dialog is kept in the story, vary pacing or use pauses for listeners to reflect on what is being said.

Bible stories are powerful. Trust the power of God's Word. Don't be afraid of shorter stories and be patient in telling longer stories while the listeners mentally try to keep up.

Don't be afraid to repeat a story if necessary. Oral communicators usually do not mind repetition, as the first time they hear a story, they do not know where it is heading or concluding. After the first time the listeners may be more relaxed and enjoy the story more as they "know" the story and so can relax a bit while listening.

If you make a minor mistake, do not interrupt the story to correct it. Listeners may not know you have made a mistake. If you make a major mistake you will need to decide whether it is worth stopping the story to correct the mistake or even to start over. I have found it helpful (because I have made mistakes) to say to the listeners, "Let me begin again. This story is so important that I must tell it correctly for you."

The Bible Storying Venue

The places or situations where you might tell Bible stories can vary considerably. It could be a conversational one-on-one encounter. It could be to a person or family in a home. It could be to a gathered crowd. And it could be to some of your own team so that the local people can "overhear" the stories and not feel threatened by a directly told story.

Obviously, in the larger venues it is difficult to conduct dialog and get replies. One way to handle this is not to use pre and post-story dialog—just tell the stories. Another is to ask questions rhetorically to provoke thought or stir interest, but not necessarily to expect listeners' reply.

When using stories with just one or two people, revert to a more conversational approach, perhaps beginning a question with "Have you ever thought about…? When storying for a very small group, the group dynamic becomes even more important than with larger gatherings. Opportunity for dialog in small groups should when possible be seized.

Use a Bible or Not?

There may be instances where it is not appropriate or allowed to use a Bible. Fortunately, these are few. A bigger problem is that an open book can distance the storyer from nonliterate listeners.

In some situations an open Bible that is a clean copy—not visibly marked—can serve to add authority as some cultures have deep respect for a holy book. If you need to use a written story, prepare one on a sheet of letter-size paper in half-page columns (landscape format) folded in half with the story printed in at least 14-point type for legibility. You might insert the page(s) in your Bible.

When and Where to Tell the Stories?

The obvious answer is when you have potential listeners. During a project, a story time might be announced and begun at a convenient time—often in the evening after eating and before bed. Local factors will provide the answer to the time question.

Some have used stories with local workers while working together. Don't be surprised if listeners ask for another story or two. Be prepared for such a request.

Find out from local workers or those who know the culture when and where true stories are told and who is qualified to tell true stories.

Who Can Tell Stories?

In many cultures the correct hair color is "white." Age denotes wisdom and authority. Visitors to an area often have an opening as guests to tell a story.

I used to ask my interpreters to tell the next story as they already knew it. But the clever ones would reply, "No, you better tell the story. The people will listen better if a foreigner tells the story and I just interpret!"

In some situations storying teams have been used with one person to do the pre-story and post-story times and another person to tell the story. It helps if others on the team also know the story and can prompt if needed.

Using Recorded Stories

There are several advantages to using a recorded story. One is that copies can be left behind to be replayed by the listeners. Compact Disc players are becoming more common. Cassette tapes may still be the universal medium. Some are now using memory stick MP3 digital players through a small sound system for their pre-recorded stories.

Another advantage is that a national or fluent missionary can make a recording from a translated script that is accurate and expressed well. When a recorded story is used, plan to do the pre-story and post-story dialog (if used) live. Recorded stories could be used in a series that is repeated. This is good for clinic or other waiting areas.

A brief story-to-story transition or introduction before stories is helpful if a normal pre and post-story dialog is not used.

One listener in northeast Thailand told a storyer that she preferred to hear the story from the (cassette) "machine" as it always told the story the same way every time!

Develop Your Own Storytelling Style

The preceding list of suggestions is based my personal experience. But no two Bible storyers will necessarily do things exactly the same way. Feel free to work out your own style. After sharing stories a few times you will develop a routine or pattern that will become progressively easier for you and appropriate for your listeners.

Many churches are sending out mission teams and response teams for ministry. It could be helpful if the team agreed on doing things generally the same way so there would be no "favorites" among the storyers.

Train a Local Storyer or Assistant

While it is good to take the Bible stories *to* a people, it is better to leave the Bible stories *with* the people. One way to help this along is to use every available opportunity to train an assistant or local storyer who can continue reviewing or even telling the new stories in your absence.

If you use an interpreter, that person is an assistant who should learn the stories through hearing and interpreting after several story sets. Encourage them to find places and people where they can tell the stories in their own sessions.

If fluent in the local language so that an interpreter is not needed, then select one of the local people who is already a believer to be your assistant. In the beginning let that person prepare the listeners for the story session. Then begin letting the assistant read the story (if literate) or tell it while you do the pre and post-story portions. As the person grows in competence allow them to review the previous stories or lead in the retelling of the present story if listeners need a retelling to help them to remember it. That assistant can then fill in on a temporary basis if you the storyer are away. This helps to keep the continuity and builds growing competence in the assistant. One practice is for you the storyer to first tell the story and then allow your assistant to retell it in their own words or as accurately as they can. They can then lead in the post-story time when the listeners are given opportunity to retell the story.

Even if a person is not yet a believer, they can still serve a useful function in reviewing previous stories as part of the pre-story time. Since you are present for this, any story drift can be caught and corrected.

Some storyers like to team story where two or more work as a team sharing in the story assignments or one telling the stories while another leads the pre and post-story time, This has worked well in some husband and wife teams.

Questions About Compiled Stories

Some who use Bible stories are uncomfortable using compiled (assembled) stories that are composed of various Bible passages pulled together into a single coherent narrative. If this is a problem for the storyer, then prepare or adapt your own preferred versions to tell. Some literate listeners could be disturbed that the stories as told cannot be found in one place in their Bible.

What I have done in such cases is to read all the source or component passages to let them see these did indeed come from the Bible, then tell the story to let them see how I have compiled or assembled a narrative from the component passages. Generally I have had no complaints after doing this.

If compiled stories from scattered references are a problem for you or your listeners, then don't use them. Rely only on the existing scripturally intact stories. Incidentally, Peter, Stephen, and even Paul compiled and paraphrased Old Testament stories that foretold Jesus that they used in their sermons.

Stories can be strengthened by linking two or more stories in a related series like an intro story, the main story, and a follow-though or closure story.

Several thematically related stories can be told in a series like The Lost Sheep, The Lost Coin and The Lost Son. Another thematic variation is to cluster several stories like those related to food or feeding, Jesus' authority to forgive sin, his authority over evil spirits, physical impairment, sickness or death. The cluster provides a strong emphasis and perhaps different facets of the same theme.

Stories can be compiled from several parallel accounts like the four versions of Feeding the 5,000 to provide a fuller account.

Talking About & Teaching From Bible Stories

Frequently Asked Questions

Some questions often arise when speaking of Bible Storying. Among these questions are:

1. What stories to tell?
2. How do I tell the stories?
3. After I tell the stories, what do I talk about?

An observation I have made with oral communicators is that many enjoy "learning" from the stories rather than being told what the stories "teach." One of the objectives is, therefore, to facilitate the listeners' learning from the stories.

In other words, let the listeners participate as much as possible in learning from the stories by involving them in an interactive dialog. *This process* helps to lead them to the truths to learn, and that helps to answer any questions they may have regarding the story and its implications. This process can involve things that are different from their culture or which challenge or clash with their cultural norms and beliefs and allow listeners to interact and resolve the differences rather than being told how they must respond.

You have chosen the stories to use with purpose. This purpose will now help to guide your discussion questions before the story and after the story.

Before the Story

Before the story you will want to:

1. *Capture the listeners' interest.* Some stories are inherently more interesting than others. Some storyers like to announce the title or what their story is about. For example the interest getter might be: "Today's story is about a prophet fed by birds and an angel." That unusual title should immediately draw some interest. In some African countries the norm is to tell the ending of the story and then tell the story to show how it happened that

way. Short previews stimulate interest to hear the future stories.

2. *Use sensitizing questions.* As a general rule sensitizing questions are asked that pose a problem or unusual situation, or that might ask a question to draw the listeners into relating to the story in some way. A good sensitizing question will typically stir up animated talk among listeners.

3. *Give only needed background information.* Many stories may also need some background information or pre-story comment to help prepare listeners for the story. Do not attempt to give more than just enough background or introduction to get the story going. Leave some room for imagination and suspense to develop. Experience will indicate when there is a need to supply more information if the listeners consistently seem confused or ask questions indicating a lack of understanding.

After the story

A Bible story should be as relational as possible—that is, connect with the listeners so that a discussion afterward is a natural result of the story. The story may pose a dilemma, or provide a situation similar to the experiences of listeners. Following are a few suggestions for developing your own discussion time:

1. *Ask questions about any essential facts or dialog between story characters.* The purpose of these questions is to review key story facts and to explore the story if that is culturally appropriate. *A word of caution*: Typically oral communicators do not deconstruct a story. They consider stories holistically—the story is a whole and may fall apart for them if broken into pieces.

2. *Oral communicators often tire easily.* Unless the listeners express an interest in talking more about a story, then limit the discussion to what they are comfortable with. In many Bible storying resources the post-story dialog questions are given as a resource to stimulate ideas for the storyer who uses that set of stories. Se-

lect, revise or adapt the suggested dialog questions to what fits your listeners best.

3. *Keep discussion questions or comments as relational as possible.* Most oral communicators live in a very relational world. They live in communities where interpersonal information is shared frequently among the community. And they will usually relate best to stories and discussion that touches their world and lives in some way. The storyer's understanding of their worldview is helpful and can be tempered with experience gained among the listeners.

4. *Lead to some personal application or implication.* The stories are not told just to entertain, but to supply information to fill in spiritual gaps or progressively lead to deeper spiritual truths with personal application or implication.

5. *Use a memory verse if appropriate.* The purpose of a memory verse can be to summarize a story or to emphasize a key truth or promise in the story. And the verse provides additional opportunity for interactive participation as the verse is repeated several times by the storyer and then several times by the listeners. Some verses (or groups of verses) may be too long to learn easily. If so, plan to read the verses several times so that listeners will have a familiarity.

As a longtime storyer let me make a general observation that women storyers may be a bit better at relational post-story discussions. As a general rule men may be better at doctrinal post-story discussions.

Do not cut off the storying time if listeners want to talk additionally about the story. Some of the best discussions I remember came from the listeners' own post-story questions and comments. Rather than overload them with more information than they are seeking, try to use another story if possible so that the story-as-source continues.

If a lengthy or detailed post-story discussion is too much for listeners, or not appropriate, then use a simple approach like the following that has worked well and is generally reproducible by listeners.

Simplified Dialog Questions

1. What part of the story do you like the best?
2. What part of the story is hard to hear or troubles you?
3. What parts of the story are hard to understand or do you have questions about?
4. What does the story say about God?
5. What part of the story would you like to tell someone else or reflect on yourself? Why?

This may provide an idea of how to word your own simple discussion questions.

Getting Response and Drawing the Net

Bible Storying used primarily for ministry objectives is first to help and heal. But it should also carry an increasingly progressive theme of pre-evangelism or evangelism. In cases of listeners living in areas where strong resistance or hostility to the Gospel commonly exists, the stories may need to emphasize the evangelism theme less until there is apparent openness. The general rule is to keep listeners listening and to have a strengthening relationship between ministry workers and listeners.

Because situations vary so greatly, it is difficult to prepare a one-size-fits-all set of Bible story lessons that is at the same sensitive to relationships and as evangelistically aggressive as possible. In cases where listeners are more neutral it is easier to err on the side of more evangelism emphasis.

Response to the Bible stories and discussion times can come unsolicited from listeners who express an interest or desire to know more, or to respond to God's Word and what they are hearing in the stories. In the case of any who are expressing an early desire to know more or to believe, take them aside and teach them from an appropriate set of evangelism scriptures and give invitation to believe in Jesus. Ask them to keep their peace as others do not yet have their understanding are not yet ready to make such a decision.

In communal situations belief may lag until a leader expresses a desire to believe. Individuals may not be culturally free to make a decision on their own. Where persecution is a possibility, it is better to wait until a group or majority are ready to profess faith in Christ.

Where the ministry stories are used primarily for ministry or pre-evangelism, the objective would be to lead listeners toward God the Creator to whom we are accountable and Jesus the Savior, and prepare them for a more aggressive evangelistic story set with the themes of broken relationship due to sin, judgment, forgiveness and the need for a Savior handled more directly. Then invite response.

Using Visuals to Tell Bible Stories

Using pictures or other visuals while telling the story, can be powerful aids to accompany Bible stories. Some storyers like pictures to attract attention. One storyer in Bangladesh was having difficulty attracting attention of Hindu women. She had a set of teaching pictures I had given her. Cleverly she posted the crucifixion picture in a prominent place. Soon the women were coming to her to say the picture disturbed them. The storyer then asked if the women would like to hear a story that told about that picture. Pictures can help to depict strange or unfamiliar scenes and concepts to listeners and stir their interest to hear more.

Some storyers prefer to display the pictures as they tell the story, and even to refer to the picture during the story. A series of pictures can depict plot progression. Pictures may relate directly to some aspect of a people's culture or activity or illustrate some unfamiliar or unusual aspect of the Bible story. Pictures can have cultural problems, so test or get local opinion before using. See *Basic Bible Storying* text for more information on typical cultural and social issues in using teaching pictures.

The size (and detail) of graphic visuals should be appropriate for the size of the typical listening audience. There are teaching pictures that come in different sizes and binding formats that would be appropriate for certain groups. For larger crowds larger pictures are needed. Storying pictures on cloth like the *Storying Scarf*[7] are helpful in small groups, but having all the pictures displayed on the cloth can be confusing as compared to displaying one picture at a time.

Also pictures along with gestures and any drama help to visualize a story, making it more memorable for listeners. The most commonly available visuals are, of course, the storyers themselves. The use of gestures, posturing (facing different directions to indicate those speaking), and movement are common and effective visuals. Costumes (usually not a full costume but a representative costume) can add a touch of interest.

I fondly recall one man in India depicting Satan as he tempted Jesus. The man placed a cloth sack on his head and pulled up the sack's corners into two horns.

Teaching objects related to things in the stories can also be useful. In the "Ee-Taow!"[8] video Mark Zook holds a lamb doll and a knife as he tells the story of sacrifice to the Mouk listeners. Previously Mark had used a map in explaining the relationship of the Mouk to the location of the Bible story. And later he had the Mouks to dramatize the arrest, trial, crucifixion, and resurrection of Jesus. One visual that was said to be particularly effective was a balloon filled with red-tinted water that was punctured under the clothing of Jesus on the cross to illustrate the shed blood.

Picture sets are probably most commonly used by non-national storyers. There are many differing sets of Bible teaching pictures, all with differing characteristics and cultural bias. Some of the effective ones I have used were the "Telling the Story…" color pictures from New Tribes Mission, Biblical Wall Posters from India, and the "Look, Listen & Live" flipcharts from Global Recordings Network. (See list of visual sources at the end of this chapter.)

Flannelgraph (felt) sets are also very effective because of the animation in building the picture from the cutouts. But the cost of pure flannel sets (more durable) is relatively high compared to flocked paper (less durable) sets. There is the matter of proper storage and cataloging of component pieces for building each scene.

These flannelgraph stories have worked best in institutional settings or where a storyer used them personally and there was not a need to train national storyers to use the flannelgraph sets. One of the most popular is the Betty Lukens *Bible in Felt* that comes in a smaller classroom size and a larger public size.

There are certain advantages to using flat (unbound) teaching pictures versus bound (flipchart) sets of pictures. The unbound set allows for easier editing or selection of the needed pictures and convenient display in a series on a line or held up one by one for review of stories. The disadvantage is potential loss of individual pictures or for some national storyers getting the pictures out of order.

The bound sets in flipchart format are generally more durable and less likely to lose individual pictures. The pictures can only be displayed one at a time rather than serially side-by-side as with unbound sets. The binding makes skipping over unneeded pictures more difficult. Having the pictures locked in the proper chronological display order is helpful and less confusing for national storyers or assistants.

One general disadvantage of all picture sets used with Bible Storying is the problem of stories with no pictures available to use or that can be borrowed from another story. Some picture sets may have cultural problems because of clothing (especially for women) and other things like portraying relationships that are not acceptable to local culture. In some cultures, any picture of "God," "Jesus," or even the prophets' faces may be inappropriate.

Where pictures are used to train local national storyers, the pictures may give a bit more boldness to younger or timid storyers as well as helping to qualify young storyers to be able to tell stories to older listeners. Teaching pictures do help to attract listeners and give support to understanding new or unusual things in stories. But one time when I was in Africa teaching Bible Storying, an older African man told me: "If you tell the stories well, you don't need any pictures!"

One major difficulty in attempting to use Bible teaching pictures with *The Food Stories* is that there are relatively few of the food stories illustrated as such. This would vary from set to set. The most common picture is Feeding of the Multitude depicting Jesus holding the bread and fish with the seated crowds. Next might be Last Supper. Moses Striking the Rock is fairly common and Israelites Gathering Manna is may also be available.

Once when I needed a picture of Ruth gleaning in the field and could not find one, I discovered a picture of Judith from the Apocrypha and simply relabeled it. Another time when all I had of Jonah was him lying on the beach with a very large fish out in the sea, I found a picture of Paul and Barnabas setting out at Joppa and another of Peter preaching to the crowd in Jerusalem and simply relabeled them to have a series of three pictures which illustrated the parts of the story better than a single picture.

Alternatives to using imported pictures exist and provide some help in storying. Because pictures can be culturally offensive or inappropriate for a number of reasons, it is sometimes best not to use them. An alternative is to look for a set of locally available Bible pictures that would probably be known by local mission or contact personnel in a country. Ask your local contact what is available.

Some storyers are now beginning to use mutually agreed upon symbols related to each picture. These are simple but identifiable symbols that can be helpful to illustrate some event or focus in a story and help to prompt recall. Those skilled in chalk drawing (chalk talk) have sketched their pictures. A few have used puppets to tell their stories. This, however, works best as a team project and may require some minimal stage equipment.

Be sure to test all picture sets before using them or ask if sets have already been in use and if there were any problems associated with using them. If you use an interpreter, they may ask you to leave the picture set with them for continued use.

For more specific information regarding culturally adapted picture sets and additional information about using them email jot2@sbcglobal,net and mention this book.

Visual Resources

1. "Telling the Story..." 105 13x17 inch color pictures of selected OT and NT stories. Pictures are painted with acrylic paints and are very life-life. Available from New Tribes Mission, Sanford, Florida. http://www.ntmbooks.com/chronological_teaching?page=3.

2. "Telling the Story..." black and white letter-size line drawings taken from the color set are less costly and may be hand colored or easily duplicated for sharing. New Tribes Mission also has these same pictures in digitized form on CD.

3. Biblical Wall Posters. 140 16x21 inch color contextualized pictures—80 OT and 60 NT. Available in Bangalore, India. National Catechetical Literature Center. The paper is a bit fragile but the set was great at a low cost.

4. "Look, Listen & Live." Eight 13x17 inch spiral bound flipcharts with 24 pictures each. Five have OT stories, two are the stories of Jesus, and one is the Acts stories. Pictures are basically bold b/w line drawings that are filled in with bright colors and so display well. Obtain from Global Recordings Network: http://globalrecordings.net/topic/audiovisuals.

5. Betty Lukens "Bible in Felt." Over 600 felt pieces and large backgrounds depicting over 150 Bible stories. Sets come in two sizes—the smaller or group size uses 6 in. figures. The larger or crowd size uses 12 in. figures. The sets are relatively expensive but do have a high attention value when used. www.http://www.thefeltsource.com/BibleStories.html?OVRAW=Bible%20Lesson%20For%20Children&OVKEY=child%20bible%20lesson&OVMTC=standard.

6. "The Storying Scarf." The Storying Scarf is a cotton muslin scarf designed to put an inexpensive set of durable pictures representing God's Word in the hands of people who could use it to independently share God's Word where missionaries cannot go. It is designed to be used

in conjunction with a series of 21 Chronological Bible stories. http://www.storyingscarf.com/

7. Kanga Cloth or West African Bible Storying Cloth. 42 color pictures on a 40x33 in. cloth. http://imbresources.org/index.cfm/fa/store.prod/ProdID/1619.cfm

8. Some churches have unused sets of Sunday School Bible teaching pictures. The older pictures which are more like paintings do not display as well as the newer simpler pictures that are b/w line drawings that are filled in with color. Check your Children's Department!

References

[1] J.O.Terry, *The Water Stories*, Church Starting Network (www.churchstarting.net)

[2] Benedicte Grima, *The Performance of Emotion Among Paxtun Women*, University of Texas Press: Austin, 1992.

[3] J.O.Terry, *The Grief Stories*, Church Starting Network. (www.churchstarting.net)

[4] Disaster Response Assistance Training, Strategic World Impact, Bartlesville, OK.

[5] J.O.Terry, *The Hope Stories*, Church Starting Network (www.churchstarting.net)

[6] J.O.Terry, *Basic Bible Storying*, Church Starting Network. (www.churchstarting.net)

[7] "Ee-Taow!", New Tribes Mission, Sanford, FL.(video)

For other books and for new releases check the Church Starting Network website www.churchstarting.net or www.Bible-Storying.com.

Additional websites which may contain helpful information are:

www.www.stroying.com and www.oralstrategies.com

For questions regarding use of this book or related Bible Storying ministry contact jot2@sbcglobal.net.

www.ingramcontent.com/pod-product-compliance
Lightning Source LLC
Chambersburg PA
CBHW050821160426
43192CB00010B/1848